BUSH PILOTS

Canada's Wilderness Daredevils

PETER BOER

FOLK
LORE
PUBLISHING

The Publisher: Folklore Publishing
Website: www.folklorepublishing.com

Library and Archives Canada Cataloguing in Publication

Boer, Peter, 1977–
    Bush pilots : Canada's wilderness daredevils / by Peter Boer.

(Legends series)
Includes bibliographical references.
ISBN 1-894864-12-3

    1. Bush pilots—Canada, Northern—History. I. Title. II. Series: Legends series (Edmonton, Alta.)

TL523.B63 2004   629.13'092'271   C2004-903087-6

Project Director: Faye Boer
Title Page: Aviation pioneers Wop May, Grant McConachie, Punch Dickins
Photography credits: Every effort has been made to accurately credit the sources of photographs. Any errors or omissions should be directed to the publisher for changes in future editions. *Photographs courtesy of* Adlair Aviation (p. 189; p. 205); Alan Bibby (p. 237); Archives of Manitoba (p. 89, C.A.L. 1527; p. 101, C.A.L. 1531; p. 113, N21154; p. 121, C.A.L. 1665; p. 217, C.A.L. 2146; p. 224, C.A.L. 2147); Canada Aviation Museum (p. 17, 2341; p. 29, 4211; p. 41, 1238; p. 79, 25927; p. 142, 7186; p. 153, 12208; p. 156, PP02-0677; p. 173, 23636); Colin Caldwell (p. 163); Glenbow Archives, Calgary, Canada (title page, NA 1258-11; p. 26, NA-1821-2; p. 34, NA-1258-119; p. 51, NA-1258-77; p. 56, NA-1258-37; p. 84, NA-463-6; p. 144, NA-463-2); Max Ward (p. 179; 183); National Archives of Canada (p. 60, C-61972; p. 69, PA-89694; p. 126, C-61896); Tracy B. Perry (p. 201); Western Canada Aviation Museum (p. 91, OS6946-47).

We acknowledge the support of the Alberta Foundation for the Arts for our publishing program.

PC: P5

Table of Contents

Acknowledgments

MY MOST HEARTFELT THANKS to the staff of the Western Canada Aviation Museum in Edmonton, Alberta, for their time, expertise and the use of their archives. To the Edmonton Public Library, for forgiving a small ransom in library fines so this book could one day see a press. To Ian Leslie at the Canadian Aviation Museum, for his advice and contacts. To Jim McAvoy, for letting me into his world and reliving the past, even though it was painful for him. To Colin Caldwell for telling me all about a father he never knew. To my father Hank, for exposing me to flight at an early age despite the mess it created. To Kate, my partner of four years, for her gentle support and patience during the writing of this book. To my coworkers at the St. Albert Gazette and all my friends, for their constant inquiries: thanks for keeping me honest. And most importantly, to my publisher, roommate and mother Faye, for believing in my ability when few had reason to do so.

Introduction

I COULD NEVER HAVE BEEN A BUSH PILOT. I have become, like most people of my age, partial to the everyday luxuries of life. I love microwave cookery, cable TV and electricity. If you left me alone in the forest to fend for myself without any supplies, you would probably find me trolling the woods three days later, malnourished and bearded, still looking for an outlet for my electric razor. I am an urbanite, somewhat bourgeois in my taste and lifestyle and comfortable in my milieu.

It is with an almost irrational envy that I offer this book, *Bush Pilots,* as a celebration of the kind of daring individual that is becoming increasingly scarce in this great country of ours.

No one who is truly courageous or humble can ever proclaim him- or herself to be such. Courage and humility can only be proven, never boasted. No one who was renowned in history as a hero ever referred to himself as courageous, nor a pioneer, a legend or an icon. Those who do seem overly enamored with their own importance and revel in their arrogance.

They have to prove the validity of their own existence instead of letting history prove it for them.

Roy Brown holds a special place in Canadian and world history. Although still disputed by those who study World War I, Brown is widely credited with having shot down Manfred von Richtofen, the "Red Baron," who decimated the Royal Flying Corps in the skies over Europe. Although the stresses of war and flying left him with a chronic upset stomach, Brown returned to Canada and became a bush pilot. He was one of the pilots charged with searching for the lost explorers of the MacAlpine party during the winter of 1929. Stranded for more than two months in the barren northlands, the pilots and engineers of the lost expedition survived a harrowing trip across the ice pack of the Arctic Ocean in the dead of winter while planes scoured the skies around them for signs of their survival. When the explorers and the rescuers finally met up and returned together to The Pas, Manitoba, Roy Brown offered the following thoughts on their ordeal to a journalist:

"All this about an epic flight and heroism is bunk. We were just doing our jobs. Flying is what we are paid to do."

Back then, pilots endured the aggravation of malfunctioning equipment, primitive living quarters and the constant threat of death for relatively low wages. Most were lucky to make three dollars an hour, but their commitment to their craft speaks of the early birth of a pop psychology that is considered modern. These men did what they loved, and money had little to do with their overall happiness.

They took satisfaction in surviving in the face of almost overwhelming odds. Landing a plane in the middle of a snowstorm, changing an engine in the middle of the dreaded Barren Lands of the Northwest Territories or hiking endless hours through the bush in search of aid were commonplace events in the lives of such great men as Grant McConachie, Max Ward and Punch Dickins. These were not just pilots. They

were mechanics, engineers, blacksmiths, carpenters, hunters
and outdoorsmen. They were problem solvers and practical
geniuses. Most importantly, they were stubborn. They could
never bring themselves to accept defeat in the face of disaster or
certain death. Instead of crumbling, these men accepted every
challenge they faced with unflappability and a cool that is now
revered and seldom practiced. There was no glory in their pursuits, no big bonuses or TV movies for having survived their
ordeals. They persevered because their existence was being put
to the test, and the only alternative was death. They had wives
they loved, daughters and sons that needed providing for and
expensive planes for which they were responsible.

These characteristics were not solely masculine. Although
they are sadly underrepresented in this book, there were several
influential women pilots who displayed exactly the same
moxie and drive as their male counterparts. Esmée Cruickshank and Jeanne Gilbert flew with their husbands on numerous trips, offering companionship and assistance in navigating
the treacherous wastelands of the North. Jeanne Gilbert, wife
of Walter Gilbert, became the first licensed female pilot in
British Columbia. Esmée, sadly, lost her husband Andy to a crash
in 1932. In the 1930s, there were no benefits or pensions for
widows of bush fliers. Esmée worked as a telephone operator
for a year to support her two children before returning to her
parents in Vancouver.

Although there were many women pilots in the 1920s and
1930s, few sought any sort of employ with their highly special-
ized skill set. Or if they did, they were routinely rejected
because of their gender. When Eileen Vollick inquired at the
Jack V. Elliot Flying School in Hamilton about flying lessons,
the male instructors were doubtful she was tall enough to see
over the windscreen of the school's aircraft. Vollick overcame
her physical limitations and became Canada's first licensed
female pilot in 1928, but it was not until the 1940s that

women began to work in the field of aviation. Like most great changing points in world history, war was the catalyst.

Because of the need for strong, young men to serve on the front lines of World War II, women were offered more opportunities for employment than ever before. They served as factory workers, munitions inspectors and clerical staff in both civilian life and the military so the men could be freed to fight the Germans. They were also given the chance to learn to fly when the Air Transport Auxiliary (ATA) was created. The ATA was responsible for ferrying aircraft of all classes and sizes throughout North America and Europe during the war, and many Canadian women piloted these great war machines to their destinations. One of these was Violet Warren, née Milstead. Her friends just called her Vi.

By war's end, Vi was qualified to fly almost every plane in the Allied air force. She ferried Hurricane, Spitfire and Mustang fighters, as well as twin-engine Mosquitos, Wellingtons and Beaufighters. She flew across Canada, England and Scotland, doing her part to support the war effort. When she returned to Canada after the war and was demobilized from the military, she was offered a job as a pilot for Nickel Belt Airways. Although it is a claim she disputes hotly to this very day, history describes her as Canada's first female bush pilot. She taught flying lessons for Nickel Belt Airways and flew charter flights throughout northern Ontario, displaying just as much iron will as the hardiest of her male colleagues. The story goes that she once kicked a gruff, hardened miner out of her airplane and into a lake after enduring many hours of sexist, ignorant comments. When the plane landed and the loudmouthed miner leaned forward for a kiss, Milstead tossed him out the cargo door and into the drink.

Post-war Canada was in need of heroes, and the pilots in this book fulfilled that need with quiet dignity and resilience. Wilfrid Reid "Wop" May, perhaps Canada's most famous bush pilot, captured the national imagination with his close encounter with the Red Baron over the skies of Europe, then added to his legend with the celebrated mercy flight of 1929.

Clennell Haggerston "Punch" Dickins cut through Canada's most isolated territories in the cockpit of his beloved Fokker SK. He slew the empty, forsaken giant of the Barren Lands and pioneered the use of the airplane to deliver mail to points in the Far North.

Harold "Doc" Oaks combined a love of flying with an education in mining to exploit Canada's most treasured resources. A dedicated, fearless man dogged by a nickname he couldn't escape, Oaks was often the last point of contact with civilization for many prospectors living abject lives of solitude.

Walter Gilbert further devoured the outreaches of the North in the cockpit of an airplane and was the first pilot to photograph the Magnetic North Pole. As if making history wasn't satisfaction enough, Gilbert also sought out the ghosts of the past by participating in a search for the remains of Sir John Franklin's expedition.

Other bush pilots moved from the high-risk, uncomfortable confines of their bush planes to become pioneers in national and international commercial flight. George William "Grant" McConachie, who became president of Canadian Pacific Airlines, one of Canada's first national carriers, got his flying start hauling 30,000 tons of whitefish from Cold Lake to Bonnyville, Alberta.

Max Ward, founder and president of the now-defunct charter air service Wardair, learned to fly in the air force and learned the tricks of being a bush pilot in Canada's Northwest Territories. Wardair, still renowned in Canadiana for its high quality of service, was Ward's third attempt at a flying business.

For as many pilots who endured in their careers and lived long, productive lives, many others died strapped into the seats of their aircraft. Frederick S. "Steve" Stevenson, celebrated for his role in the WCA airlift that established rail service to Fort Churchill, Manitoba, crashed twice in his short flying career. He survived the first with broken bones. He died instantly in the second.

The mystery of the disappearance of Charles Malcolm "Chuck" McAvoy was finally solved in 2003. A hardened northerner with questionable judgment, McAvoy disappeared on a flight in 1964 in weather that grounded the hardiest bush pilots of the day. The discovery of his wreckage and corpse in the North's Barren Lands made headlines in newspapers across North America.

Although Colin S. "Jack" Caldwell started out as an airplane mechanic in the Canadian air force, he soon became a pilot as well. Sadly, a freak collision with a newly strung power line ended his young life at 32, three weeks shy of the birth of his first son.

Each chapter stands as evidence of the toughness and mental agility each of these men brought to bush flying, but no story, no exploit better personifies their mettle than that of the MacAlpine expedition and search of 1929. A group of eight pilots and engineers on a flight for Dominion Explorers Ltd. spent three months stranded in the North, surviving off meager rations and spoiled fish. The resulting search by the rest of the aviation community was, at the time, the largest in history.

With every success in bush flying, however, came tragedy. When Punch Dickins got his first job as a pilot with Western Canada Airways, there were no surviving pilots over the age of 30. The parachute was a novelty in the late 1920s, and the wireless radio did not become standard issue on airplanes until well past that time. Instrumentation was limited, and in the North, the weather could change in a moment. Planes were built to fly, not to survive a crash, and many promising young men died as a result. Fred Stevenson, Chuck McAvoy and Jack Caldwell are three men documented in this book who gave their lives to flying and lost them because of it. Dozens more suffered the same fate, some were found later and laid to rest, and others' spirits still prowl the skies of the North.

History needs the perspective of an outsider. Its most important figures cannot fully appreciate their own importance when examining their own lives. People's lives and events require context and political and social detail in order for us to fully recognize the magnitude of a life, an achievement or even a catastrophe.

A veteran bush pilot may be able to provide more specific, technical detail than can I in the scope of this book, but it would ultimately be underlined by the belief that these men were just doing their jobs. I agree that they were doing only what was asked of them, but they did it in the most spectacular way. The pilots described in this book pushed geographical and social boundaries. They opened up whole new worlds to travel and commerce, helped unearth some of our world's most priceless treasures, shuttled food, medicine and supplies to the sick and destitute and scoured the land for lost pilots or explorers. They came to know our Native peoples better than any of us could claim, and they pried the lid off the vacuous, empty reaches of the North. Our country flourished as a result of their efforts.

Their accomplishments should not be dismissed as just work and should be celebrated for the enormity of their impact and achievement. The courage and humility of these dauntless flyers should be proven.

CHAPTER ONE

Wilfrid Reid "Wop" May

1896–1952

IN −60° F WEATHER, THE MAN WAS BURNING UP. Dr. Harold Hamman withdrew his hand and scribbled on his notepad. Next he reached out and felt his patient's neck, even though he didn't need to. It was engorged. The lymph nodes were inflamed and rigid.

He reached around and grabbed a nearby lantern, holding it overhead as he pulled at his patient's chin to look down his throat. The flickering light of the oil flame glistened off a waxy coating on the man's tonsils that was creeping down his esophagus. All the signs were there. There was no doubt about it now.

Diphtheria.

Hamman had been summoned to Little Red River, Alberta, by a letter from the wife of Mr. Logan, the manager of the Hudson's Bay Company in the community. When Hamman arrived, he found Logan still in bed, sweating in the biting chill of the northern winter and fighting for air with each gasp. The fever, the swollen glands and now the waxy membrane in his throat confirmed the presence of diphtheria, a disease so contagious that it could wipe out an entire town in a matter of weeks.

And weeks was how long it would take to get the serum. Hamman was the only doctor in the area of Little Red River, a settlement northeast of Fort Vermilion, Alberta. He already knew the status of his medical supplies: he had the serum for diphtheria, but it was old and likely ineffective by now. Even if it was still viable, he did not have enough to treat the epidemic he feared, nay, he *knew* was coming.

Logan had been out and about during the days before, coughing and breathing on everyone around. His son was already feverish and achy. The bacteria could decimate the town, and Hamman felt powerless to stop it.

His only hope was to get a message to Edmonton to the Ministry of Health and beg them to send more serum. But the nearest telegraph station was in Peace River, which was two weeks away by dogsled. And even if he got the message to Peace River, it would take even longer to get the serum from Edmonton to Little Red River. By the time the serum arrived, it would be too late for the people of that tiny community.

But Hamman knew he had to at least try. Writing quickly in the flickering candlelight of the Logan home, Hamman dashed off a quick telegram, then grabbed his coat and hurried over to a nearby house. He passed the message off to two local men, Joe Lafleur and William Lambert, who agreed to take the telegram to Peace River by horse team for transmission.

Hamman watched the sleigh skate across the snowy North the next morning. Barring any difficulty, they could get to Peace River and transmit the message. But what good would it do? How could they possibly get the serum to him in time?

⚜

Wilfrid Reid May was born on March 20, 1896, in Carberry, Manitoba. Named for Canada's seventh prime minister, Wilfrid Laurier, May was an inquisitive, energetic youth. He worried his mother because he often disappeared until after sunset, exploring the world around his parents' home, only to return caked in dirt, grass and twigs and carrying some sort of animal in his arms. He was raised in a middle-class household; his father, Alexander, was the owner of a local implement shop and later became the mayor of Carberry.

But Alexander May had his sights set on federal politics, and with no seat available in Carberry, he decided to pull up roots and move his family west to Edmonton, North-West Territories, in 1903. (Alberta became a province in 1905.) As they traveled to Edmonton, the Mays stopped to visit relatives. During one of these visits, young Wilfrid was playing with one of his cousins, a two-year-old girl who was having difficulty pronouncing his name. Try as she might, all that came out was "Wop." His family, strangely delighted by the nickname, began to use it, too. They may as well have changed his birth certificate because, for the rest of his life, Wilfrid would be known first and foremost as Wop.

While growing up in Edmonton, May was exposed to a variety of experiences. His father opened a service station, and after school, May helped his father work on cars. By the time he was a teenager, May had become an adept mechanic, not only repairing motors but working to make them better, faster and more powerful. With a keen mind and a proven ability to solve problems, Wop became a dependable mechanic, and his father was proud of him.

But in 1910, May's eyes lit on the one thing to which he would devote the rest of his life. In 1910, an airplane came to Edmonton for the first time. May stood in the crowd of the exhibition grounds, watching as the already-ancient Curtis Pusher delighted the crowds with its swoops and loops and spins. His mind soared with the plane, conjuring ideas of travel and freedom, of joy and delight, of flying. Those thoughts and images endured throughout his youth and his years at Western Canada College in Calgary.

One day, while walking to class, May walked by a newspaper stand where he saw, on the front page, a photo of a fighter plane in action over the skies of Europe. It was 1915; the Great War was not yet a year old, but in that instant, May knew his destiny. He was bound for Europe. He would learn to fly in the skies above France.

However, dreams and reality are rarely in sync. When May first enlisted in the armed forces, the Canadian military had no air force and no procedure for training pilots. Instead, May was posted to the 202nd City of Edmonton regiment as a staff sergeant. He became a machine-gunner, mowing down hordes of German troops who stormed the trenches of the Canadian and British armies. Throughout the conflict, May let his intentions to fly be known to anyone who would listen to him. He watched as swarms of planes met like bees in the air, diving at one another, some falling to the ground in flames. He wanted more than anything to be up there with them, and he pleaded with his superiors for the opportunity. In November 1917, he was transferred to the Royal Flying Corps and was shipped out to its school of instruction in England.

For the first few days, they did little but taxi about in their Caudron G3s, steering, braking and learning to work the controls. On November 17, when May was finally instructed to take off, he seized the opportunity. He soared into the air flawlessly, and for the first time, he felt the wind in his teeth as he looked down at the ground that stretched out endlessly before him. When his instructor, who was sitting behind him in the plane, ordered him to land, May didn't listen. He pulled up from his landing path, zoomed into the air once more, looped around the field and completed a figure-eight maneuver, his laughter drowning out the angry shouts of his instructor. He landed flawlessly, taxied to a stop and then turned proudly to his instructor, awaiting some sort of glowing praise

Wilfrid Reid "Wop" May poses for this photo in his parka.

for his stunning airmanship. He was confined to quarters as punishment.

By March, May had completed the requisite courses in flying, navigation, gunnery and machinery and was ready to join the battle. His first stop was the British air base at St. Omar, just west of the Belgian border. It was there that replacement pilots gathered before being posted to bases on the front. Until then, they were expected to participate in reconnaissance flights.

Shortly after arriving, May learned that he was to be posted to the 9th Naval Squadron at Bertangles, France.

But in a moment of bad judgment, May and his classmates decided to celebrate their posting to the front in several small towns on the French countryside where drink and the company of women were available. When May lurched back to base two days later, he was met by a furious Officer Commanding, Major Butler, who informed him in no uncertain terms that, because of his actions, May was to return to the pilots' pool at St. Omar forthwith.

Shocked and shamed, May left the OC's office dejected, eyes downcast, boots shuffling in the dirt. As he rounded the corner of the building, he collided with another soldier who was walking quickly.

"I'm sorry, sir—" May stammered, raising a hand to salute. As he brought his eyes up, his gaze came to rest on a familiar face. It was Roy Brown, a childhood friend from Edmonton. He and May had attended Victoria High School together and had lost contact some years before.

Brown, now a captain in the Royal Flying Corps, listened to his friend's story of carousing and poor common sense and told May he would see what he could do. After a lengthy discussion, Brown persuaded Major Butler to post May to Brown's squadron, the 209th Squadron at Bertangles.

"He's your problem now, if you want him that badly," the OC grumbled, signing the order for May's transfer. When Brown emerged waving the piece of paper in hand, May breathed a heavy sigh of relief.

"I won't let you down, Roy…I mean, sir," he said, saluting.

Brown laughed, clapped his friend on the back and guided him off to his future.

May's enthusiasm was quickly tempered by the realities of war. Millions were dying in the muck that was the battleground of Europe. In the skies, aircraft and pilots were in high demand as Germans and British rushed to feed the body machine of the aerial battlefield. Planes were constructed of wood and canvas and often broke down in mid-flight for reasons unrelated to combat. There were no flak jackets and no parachutes or ejection seats for pilots. If a plane went down, the pilot went with it, and few survived the fiery crashes that dotted the French countryside.

For this reason, Brown was cautious with the rookie pilots in his squadron. With so many rookies being blotted out of the sky on their first missions, Brown told May that he was to do nothing on his first few flights. He was to stay to the side of any dogfight—keep to the outer limits of an engagement and just observe. He was, under no circumstances, to enter battle until Brown gave him the order.

Brown knew a thing or two about flying. A seasoned veteran and fighter pilot with 12 kills to his credit, Brown suffered from chronic nausea because of the war. When he and his men returned from a successful engagement, and they cracked open bottles of whiskey to toast their return, Brown would reach instead for a cup of milk.

On April 21, 1918, May took off on his first flight with Brown and the rest of the 209th. As the flight of Sopwith Camels achieved its cruising altitude and made for the front, Brown spotted a group of German Albatross D-5s in the distance, slightly below his own planes. He turned to May and pointed at him, reminding May that he was to stay out of the fight. Then he raised a hand in the air, signaling the rest of his squadron to follow him. They dove to engage the enemy.

May circled the outskirts of the dogfight, watching British and German planes twist and bend, dive and spin, all in an effort to get a bead on each other. The rattle of machine guns split the air, and soon planes began to fall from the cloud of angry machines. May continued to circle the battle's limits, straining against Brown's orders not to engage.

Then a German Albatross peeled off from the battle below him, and May could no longer obey Brown's order. He dove on the plane, opening up with his machine guns, but the plane zipped left and headed back into the fray. May unwittingly followed, keeping his guns trained on the Albatross. He lost it for a moment, then reacquired his target and fired. He was so close that he could see the German pilot slump forward over the controls as bullets tore into him. As May banked away from his prey, he watched the German plane fall like a stone and disappear in a puff of smoke and flame on the ground below.

But now May was in trouble. His enthusiasm had overpowered his training, and in the thrill of the hunt, he had left his machine guns firing for too long. Now they were jammed, and all May could do was dive away from the dogfight, flying as fast as he could for the safety of his base. As he opened up the distance between himself and the engagement, he began to shake with excitement and relief. He had survived first contact with the enemy and even scored his first kill. He would live to fight another day.

But the Red Baron was waiting.

When other pilots spoke of him, it was in whispered tones of awe and wonder. Baron Manfred von Richtofen, dubbed the Red Baron, was Germany's most skilled pilot and the preeminent ace of the aerial battlefield. He had amassed a total of 80 kills, far and away the most of any pilot in the war. So steeped in celebrity was his reputation that he flew his own distinctive plane, a triplane Fokker VII, painted red. He was feared above all other pilots in the air and deserving of that status.

His tactics, some felt, were dishonorable. Richtofen rarely engaged directly in a dogfight or in one-on-one combat. The Red Baron preferred to circle above any aerial battle and wait for wounded planes to peel away. It was then that the Baron would pounce, diving out of the sun's blinding glare at his unsuspecting prey. Few had a chance, and fewer still ever knew what hit them before they spiraled into the ground. The Baron was the bully of the battlefield, picking on the weak and lame, and the Allied pilots hated him for it.

And so May turned to look behind him as bullets began to zing around his head, and his blood froze in his veins as his eyes locked on the red triplane of the Red Baron diving in on him. Pushing the throttles of his Camel wide open, May began to twist, turn and spin, banking left and right, up and down, trying to stay out of the torrent of lead the Red Baron was throwing at him. He dove for the ground, pulling up barely 50 feet from the treetops and trying to open up the distance between himself and his pursuer. Spying the valley of the Somme River below, he dove towards it, hoping to use its winding path as cover. But the Baron was one step ahead of him. He flew straight on, looking to cut May off at the crest of the hills of the valley. May swallowed in trepidation, desperately looking for another way out.

Suddenly, the red Fokker seemed to shake in midair. It twisted and gently nosed over, arcing in an almost-graceful dive straight towards the ground. May watched in fascination as the Baron made no attempt to pull up. The Fokker smashed into the ground below and exploded in a burst of flame.

May flinched as the roar of another airplane reached his ears. He looked to his right and saw Roy Brown, his school chum, now his savior, flying towards him. Roy Brown had shot down the Red Baron over Allied territory.

Once his body was recovered by the Allies from the crash site, the Allied airmen held a solemn ceremony for Manfred von Richtofen that evening at the British air base in Bertangles, France, where his body lay in state. Although an enemy, the Red Baron was the envy of his peers, and hundreds came to pay homage to his memory. His aircraft was scoured for mementos and good luck charms, and May retrieved a piece of the Fokker's strut. He knew he was lucky to have survived his close call and vowed before the Baron's grave that he would be more watchful in the future.

True to his promise, May racked up a total of 13 kills during the war, and he was awarded the Distinguished Flying Cross for having been shot in the line of duty. While strafing enemy troops on a mission, May was struck in the arms and face by small pieces of flak from ground fire, but he still managed to get his plane home. Not until the end of the war, however, did he allow doctors to remove the metal shards embedded in his skin. He was needed on the battlefield, and time spent recovering from surgery was time he simply didn't have to spare until the war was over.

At the end of the war, May returned home to continue what he had learned to do in the skies above France—to fly. His brother Court had started a small flying business, leasing a Curtiss Jenny from the city of Edmonton for $25 per month. Wop and Court began to barnstorm across Alberta, performing aerial stunts and putting on shows at fairs all across the province. On July 12, 1919, May stunned the crowd at the opening of Edmonton's Diamond Ball Park when, with Edmonton mayor Joe Clarke as his passenger, he flew under the High Level Bridge and over the pitcher's mound at the park so that the mayor could throw out the first pitch from the plane.

It was the first of many feats May would accomplish with May Airplanes Ltd. The Mays hired World War I veteran George Gorman as a second pilot and Pete Derbyshire as their engineer. As an advertising stunt, the *Edmonton Journal* hired Gorman to fly copies of its newspaper to Wetaskiwin 30 miles away, but he was forced to ditch the plane in a muddy farmer's field owing to poor weather. Weeks later, seeking to one-up its competition, the *Edmonton Bulletin* hired Gorman to drop 2000 copies of its newspaper on a group of the United Farmers of Alberta who were out picnicking. May and Gorman were just beginning to think about branching out into the business of airfreight and aerial photography when Imperial Oil came calling.

In the Roaring Twenties, Alberta was teeming with oil, so much black gold that the slime oozed from the ground into nearby creeks and rivers. The problem was getting at it. Moving men and materiel could be done by steamboat in the summer, but not in winter. With the cold of November holding all of Alberta in its frosty grip in 1920 and dozens of companies ready to rush north by boat come spring, Imperial Oil decided to gamble on two planes from New York and two pilots from Edmonton. May and Gorman were hired to fly two Junkers JL-6 airplanes from New York back to Edmonton so that Imperial Oil could start moving its men and machinery in before the rest of the pack.

After taking the train to New York, Gorman and May set out for home in the newest all-metal monoplanes. They passed through Sandusky, Cleveland, Chicago and Minneapolis before crossing the border into Canada. They were held up for hours, sometimes for weeks, by mechanical problems and bad weather, but on January 15, 1921, May descended from the sky into a field just outside Edmonton where almost 5000 people awaited him. They had listened to updates on his progress over the radio and thought him to be a celebrity for the flight he was making. But it was as far as May went with that particular venture.

Upon emerging from his cockpit to a chorus of cheers, questions and flashbulbs, May removed his helmet and told everyone, "I'm going to sleep. Possibly forever. Good evening, gentleman."

May severed his connection with Imperial Oil and returned to May Airlines to continue barnstorming and shipping. In May 1921, his personal life suffered a terrible blow when his brother Court fell to his death from the stairs of the Macdonald Hotel in Edmonton. Inwardly shattered, May kept on with the

business of flying, delighting crowds in the summer and working as a mechanic in the winter. In 1923, he sold his business
to Great Northern Services Ltd., but he stayed on as a mechanic
and pilot.

In November 1924, Wop married Violet Bode, whom he
met at a horse jumping show in which she was competing. Just
before her turn, he gave her his good luck charm, a wooden
monkey that he kept with him at all times. She proceeded to
knock over every obstacle on the course, and she returned
May's monkey without so much as a thank-you. But days later
they met again at the City Commissioner's office where Violet
worked as a receptionist. May courted her enthusiastically and
eventually won her over. They were married on November 19,
1924, to much fanfare because May was considered a local
celebrity. Although Violet enjoyed the wedding day, she could
not enjoy the wedding feast, for she had lockjaw from a case
of tetanus.

Now married, May looked for more regular employment
to support his bride, and he found it with National Cash Reg-
ister (NCR) in Dayton, Ohio. One day while he was working
on a metal lathe, a small metal shard shot out from the
machinery and struck May in the eye. Even though the shard
was later removed, May's vision was significantly impaired.
Others in his situation might have seen it as a sign that he was
not to fly again, but May did not. He had been itching to fly for
some time—from the day he left Edmonton he had been long-
ing for it. He missed it more than he thought he would, and
when NCR transferred him back to Edmonton, May resolved
to dedicate his life to flying.

With several local flying enthusiasts and support from the
Canadian government, May formed the Edmonton and Northern Alberta Aero Club, becoming its first president and chief
pilot. With no one in the club qualified to give flying lessons,
May resigned from NCR and headed for Moose Jaw, where he

completed a course in pilot instruction. The Edmonton club
eventually received aircraft from the Canadian government,
and May began giving lessons. The city even established an
airfield south of the city in 1928 for the club's use. The landings
were sometimes rough and the maneuvers sometimes frightening, but May was a skilled instructor and mechanic who
worked tirelessly to keep both his planes and the men under
his instruction safe.

On January 1, 1929, Dr. M.R. Bow, the Deputy Minister of
Health for the Province of Alberta, received an urgent telegram
from Harold Hamman, a doctor in Fort Vermilion:

"DIPHTHERIA. FEAR EPIDEMIC. SEND ANTITOXIN."

The manager of the Hudson's Bay Company and his wife
had contracted the highly contagious illness, and Dr. Hamman
did not have the antitoxin with which to cure them or the hundreds of others who could also fall sick. Hamman had raced by
dogsled to Fort Vermilion, where he had convinced two locals
who owned a horse team and sleigh to take the message to
Peace River. The journey by sleigh had taken 12 days. It had
been over two weeks since the original diagnosis, and it would
take even longer to get the serum 600 miles north from
Edmonton to Little Red River. By the time it got there, the
whole settlement could be wiped out.

Bow put down the message, his mind racing, and walked
over to the telephone. When the operator picked up, he asked
to be put through to Wop May. May and mechanic Vic Horner
agreed without hesitation to fly the serum to Little Red River.

The odds were against them. Their aircraft, a tiny Avro
Avian, was an open cockpit biplane with no heater, meaning
both pilot and mechanic would be exposed to temperatures
that often plunged below −60° F. There were no skis for the
Avian in all the city of Edmonton, so they would have to land

Wop May and Vic Horner, about to take off on their mercy flight from Edmonton to Fort Vermilion, 1929

~⊙✕⊙~

on wheels in the snow-choked lands and frozen lakes of the North. If they crashed, the serum crashed with them, as would the hopes of the settlers at Little Red River.

Keeping the serum warm was another matter. If it froze, it would be ruined, making the whole trip useless. The package of 600,000 units of serum, enough to treat 200 people, was wrapped in blankets and placed next to a small charcoal heater in the storage compartment of the plane. The chance of fire was high, but it seemed the only recourse.

May hopped into the plane and started it, waiting for Horner to jump in. Suddenly, Vi rushed out of the crowd towards the plane, waving at him. He leaned over, expecting tears and instead saw a smile of pride. In her hand, she held some chocolate bars.

"I'll be home before you know it," he told Vi, smiling.

May took the chocolate bars from her outstretched hand and leaned down to kiss her.

"Ready, Vic?" he shouted over his shoulder.

"Don't suppose it could wait until summer, eh?" Horner replied. May laughed, opened the throttles to full power and taxied down the runway, setting off for Fort Vermilion.

It took all May's skill and strength to keep the plane in the air. Wrapped in multiple layers of fur and cloth, he still felt the chill of the −65° F weather seep into his skin. The winds cut through them like a knife's edge, with sharp ice crystals whipping at their faces until they bled. Flying at 500 feet, visibility was sometimes zero, and May had to wipe at his goggles constantly to keep them clear. They were aloft for four hours when they finally broke out of the fog and found themselves at McLennan Junction, just south of Peace River.

Had May's forehead not been frozen, his eyebrows would have leaped up in surprise at what he saw. An airfield marked by flags had been set out for them just outside of the town. A group of men on the side of the field waved and jumped, and May banked to line up with the improvised airfield. Slowly, limbs stiff from immobility and the bone-chilling cold, May and Horner dismounted from the plane. As it turned out, Leon Giroux, a McLennan Junction resident had been tracking May's progress on his radio set and had decided to set up the landing strip in case May and Horner needed to stop. With darkness falling on the North, May and Horner gladly accepted the Giroux's offer of a warm house and a bed. They had come 267 miles that day and still had another 320 to go.

Early the next morning, they waved their goodbyes and thanks to their host. They made Peace River by noon, again able to land on an airfield hastily prepared by residents who were tracking the progress of the mercy flight by radio. Pausing only for gas and a quick thaw next to a charcoal stove, they hopped back into the plane and set off for Fort Vermilion. They had tucked the scrum inside their clothing to keep it warm. The package, as feared, had caught fire, and the pair had been forced to land to extinguish it. Just outside Peace River, a storm began to buffet their tiny biplane with its gale-force winds, and shards of ice cut open their faces. Undaunted, May kept the plane on course, and at 4:30 PM, sighed in relief as Fort Vermilion came into view. His head thick with fatigue and cold, bleeding openly from parts of his face he could no longer feel, May set the plane down beside a waiting crowd of people that included Dr. Hamman. Hands reached into the aircraft and pulled May and Horner from the plane. The two were so frozen from the flight that they couldn't even move. After a pause for a photo to mark the historic occasion, Hamman dashed off on his sled for Little Red River. It was too late to save the manager of the Hudson's Bay Company, but the serum that May and Horner delivered prevented an epidemic that could have wiped out the entire community.

On January 6, the pair returned to Edmonton to a hero's welcome. A crowd of thousands gathered at Blatchford Field to watch the pair land. They were frostbitten, covered in angry welts and sores, and May swore to Horner that he would never be warm again. Vi helped him from his aircraft to where the mayor was waiting for them. Horner and May were each awarded a gold watch for their heroic efforts, but May was just happy to be home.

May quickly forgot the cold when Cy Becker offered him a job with Commercial Airways Ltd. After flying south to California to pick up the company's new Lockheed Vega, May set to work hauling men and materiel across the West and setting records as he went. On May 24, 1929, May made the first-ever

Vic Horner (front) and Wop May pose in the Avro Avian they flew to Fort Vermilion on their mercy flight in 1929.

nonstop flight between two cities in Canada when he flew from Edmonton to Winnipeg. On September 6, May raced the fastest train in the entire North on a delivery trip. By the time May had made the delivery and returned home, the train had only just reached its destination.

The mercy flights continued as well. May flew a shipment of emergency food to 120 residents of Peace River who were

stranded by heavy spring rains that pushed the river over its
banks. He flew an oxygen tank to Fairview for a farmer with
pneumonia and then took a mentally deranged woman, her
newborn child and their doctor to Edmonton for care. May
understood the good he could do with his plane and his ability. When someone came calling for his help in an emergency,
May gave it freely.

In December 1929, May flew farther north than any pilot
had ever flown when he and a flight of four planes from Commercial Airways Ltd. left Fort McMurray for Aklavik, Yukon Territory. Aklavik was as far north as you could go on mainland
Canada. It could be called a coastal town because it was located
on the coast of the Arctic Ocean. Inhabited mostly by Hudson's
Bay Company (HBC) traders and Inuit, the isolated fort
received one mail delivery per year. May hoped to change that
when he took off from Fort McMurray with his flight of four
planes hauling five tons of mail for Aklavik and all points in
between. They stopped at Fort Resolution, Fort Smith and
other settlements along the way to deliver mail. The planes that
disgorged their entire cargo at these stops turned for home, but
May was determined to reach Aklavik and so continued on. He
spent Christmas Day at Fort Good Hope, NWT, in an abandoned cabin with his engineer and the crew of one of the other
planes. The men cracked open a bottle of rum that had been
stowed on board and made turkey stew from a frozen turkey Vi
had pressed on May before he left. Their noisy celebrations
attracted the attention of several Natives, who dropped by to
see what was going on. The result was a Christmas celebration
that May would look back on as one of the most memorable
of his life.

The crew drew on fuel caches strategically placed along their
flight path and found the remainder of the trip to Aklavik
uneventful. When they arrived, a three-day celebration ensued.
What would have normally taken two months by dog team

had taken a little over two weeks by plane. There was feasting, drinking and dancing in celebration of the delivery, and May gave rides to the Inuit, none of whom had ever flow before. While he expected them to be afraid like most people were their first time in the air, the Inuit simply sat quietly in the passenger's seat and stared out the window.

May's trip to Aklavik earned him a contract to fly mail into the North from Fort McMurray, servicing Aklavik three times a year. For his pioneering trip to Aklavik, May became the third recipient of the McKee Trophy, after Doc Oaks and Punch Dickins, for his advancement of aviation in Canada's North.

Even though he had pioneered another first, his adventures didn't stop there. In December 1931, a Native trapper stumbled into the barracks of the Royal Canadian Mounted Police in Aklavik, complaining that he had found his traps ruined and hung from a nearby tree. He suspected it was the work of another trapper in the area, a recluse named Albert Johnson who had a cabin just off the Rat River three miles from Fort McPherson, NWT. Constable King and Special Constable Bernard set off by dog team for the cabin, which was 80 miles south of Aklavik. When they arrived at the cabin and called to Johnson to come out and explain himself, they got no answer. They returned to Aklavik for a warrant and headed back to the cabin. This time a volley of rifle fire met them. Constable King was hit in the chest by one of the rounds and lay bleeding in the snow. Bernard wasted no time in lashing King to his dogsled and setting off for Aklavik. He returned days later with nine more officers and a guide. The situation was now far more serious than the simple destruction of traps. Johnson had shot a policeman.

When the posse arrived, they were greeted with the same response that King and Bernard had received—volley after volley of rifle shots. Edging his way up to the cabin, Constable McDowell threw a stick of dynamite beside the cabin and curled up in the snow as it exploded, showering everyone with dirt, snow and wood. Even though the cabin was destroyed, when McDowell raised his head, he was forced to duck again as more shots rang out.

Unsettled, the patrol headed back to Aklavik for more supplies. When they returned to Rat River five days later, they found the cabin empty and a set of tracks in the knee-high snow leading away. The hunt was on.

Following the trapper's tracks in the snow, the Mounties began a 48-day pursuit that took them into the Richardson Mountains of the Yukon. The officers were puzzled as they tracked Johnson, now dubbed by radio journalists as the "Mad Trapper of Rat River." He was moving quickly, yet did not seem to have any supplies with which to sustain himself, nor were the police dogs able to find his scent. Johnson often led them in circles as he backtracked, then followed herds of caribou to mask his footsteps. One day, while the Mounties were looking for more tracks, a single shot rang out from the trees, and Constable Spike Millen fell to the ground, dead from a gunshot wound. The Mad Trapper had graduated to murder.

At the end of January, the officers agreed that they would need a little extra help in their search efforts. They put in a call to Canada Airways Ltd. for the use of a plane and pilot to keep the team supplied and track the elusive Mad Trapper. May was eager to respond, heading north with mechanic Jack Bowen and Constable William Carter, Constable Millen's replacement.

May worked the skies above the forested lands of the Yukon, looking for any tracks or movement that might signal the Mad Trapper's whereabouts. He airlifted patrols to various locations throughout the mountains, hoping to get ahead of Johnson and cut him off. On February 17, May circled low over the Eagle River and spotted a figure dug into the snow. As he watched, and Jack Bowen took pictures, other men swarmed the figure in the middle of the Eagle River. One man went down, but the rest continued towards the one figure that lay prone. May watched in morbid fascination as the figure jerked again and again, then lay still while the other dots milled around him.

Banking swiftly, May put his plane down beside the gathered group and saw the bullet-riddled corpse of the Mad Trapper. But there was little time for gawking or reflection. Sergeant Hersey had been hit during the gun battle and needed medical attention. May fought heavy winds and snow as he made for Aklavik at his fastest possible speed. He got Hersey back to Aklavik in time to be saved and then returned to the Eagle River, where he faced the grisly task of flying the corpse of Albert Johnson to Aklavik. May wondered, like many others, who Johnson really was. The contents of his pockets—$2000, some in American currency, several gold fillings and a single pearl—raised more questions than supplied answers.

The chase completed, May returned to Fort McMurray to continue his work for Canadian Airways. In 1934, Punch Dickins, another aviation pioneer, made May the Superintendent of the Mackenzie River District, in charge of the company's flying for the entire North. It was busy work as more and more mining companies raced north to look for minerals and oil. May's planes hauled men, equipment and supplies for dozens of different companies and took on increasingly difficult challenges, such as flying entire Ford trucks to waiting camps!

"In the North, gentlemen, we are ready and able to move anything, no matter how high we have to move them," May told one radio reporter in a 1938 interview.

At home, May's life grew increasingly busy with the birth of his first son in 1935. Although Denny brought much joy into his father's life, that joy was not enough to mask a painful reality. Throughout the years, the eye that had been injured when he worked for NCR had deteriorated. His vision was failing, and the injury caused him tremendous pain. In 1937,

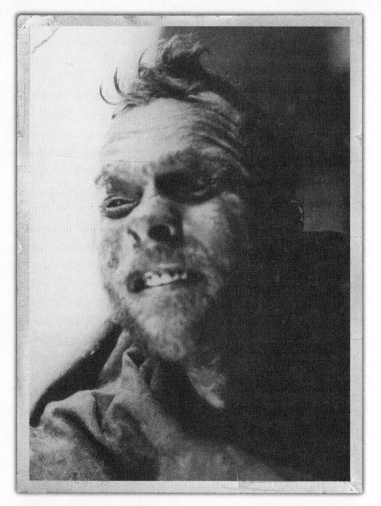

The death photo of Albert Johnson, the "Mad Trapper of Rat River," 1932. Even though he fled his cabin on foot without any tent, bedroll, stove or supplies, Johnson still managed to elude the authorities for almost two months. To this day, authorities and historians have not been able to determine exactly who Johnson was or why he behaved the way he did.

May relented and had the eye removed. He was effectively grounded. The injury had been a secret for so many years, but now there was no denying it. The glass eye that was put in its place looked real enough, but it couldn't keep May in the sky.

May made the most of his situation. The next Christmas, he presented a package to Kay Dunlop, a family friend. Her pleasure turned to horror as she unwrapped the gift and found a glass eye staring back at her. May laughed as Dunlop screamed, but he later apologized.

By 1939, the world was at war again. Having successfully invaded Poland and the Netherlands, Adolph Hitler's military juggernaut chased British troops out of France at Dunkirk. Europe was completely in the hands of the Axis powers of Germany and Italy. While the Allies of Great Britain and Canada worked to build up enough manpower to invade Europe, they began bombing German positions from the air. Lancaster and B-26 Marauder bombers supported by Hurricane fighters dropped thousands of bombs onto German military formations, factories and command centers. The strategy was costly, not just financially, but in manpower as well. German fighters and anti-aircraft fire swarmed Allied bombing raids, cutting dozens of planes out of the air at a time. Thousands of airmen never returned from their bombing missions.

To keep enough trained pilots in the air, the Allies established air combat schools in Canada. Wop May was charged with managing the operation of Observer School No. 2 in Edmonton. Recruits spent four weeks in basic training, 12 weeks learning to fly and six weeks learning bombing and gunnery. May managed the entire program, working hard to keep it challenging. These were, after all, his boys, and many of them came to his house for dinner or coffee. The program churned out over 2200 aircrews each month for the duration of the war. Many of them never returned home.

In 1941, at age 45, the stress of the war and his smoking
habit caught up to May, and he suffered a heart attack. Confined to a wheelchair for months, May began to reconnect with
his wife and family, now numbering four with the birth of his
daughter Joyce in 1939. Despite his ailing heart, he and Vi
smoked together in the evenings, and during the day he
watched Denny and Joyce as they played. When he was well
enough to return to work, he worked harder than before at
staying in touch with his family. When he was out of town, he
wrote letters and returned with gifts for Vi and the children.

In 1941, the Germans launched Operation Barbarossa, the
invasion of the Soviet Union. When Secretary General Josef
Stalin heard that Germany had invaded Russia, he responded
by locking himself in his bedroom for a week. By the time he
emerged and gave orders, the German Luftwaffe had knocked
the Russian air force out of the sky and destroyed their bases
and planes on the ground.

The Allies knew they needed to support Russia if there was
a hope of ever defeating Hitler's Germany. They began to ship
weaponry overseas, including guns, ammunition, jeeps and
eventually airplanes. Bombers and fighters were flown via
Edmonton to Alaska and then across the Bering Sea to Russia.
But many of these planes crashed en route, and survivors were
seldom found, especially in winter. This bothered May, and he
began to formulate a plan for an aerial rescue team that could
respond to news of a crash. He saw trained corpsman, maybe
even doctors, parachuting to crash sites with supplies, medicine and equipment to help save the lives of the pilots and
crews. He put his dream into action, soliciting the help of the
American parachuting school at Missoula, Montana, to train
his search-and-rescue crews. His model for aerial rescue survived for decades in both the American and Canadian mili-
taries. The idea proved so successful that the U.S. government
awarded May the American Medal of Freedom in 1947.

When the war finally ended, May remained close to his family. He devoted his summers to camping with his children, teaching them how to survive off the land and taking them on long business trips. In 1949, Canadian Pacific Airways (formerly Canadian Airways) sent him to Vancouver to negotiate commercial flight contracts with foreign countries. May reached agreements with officials in Fiji, Singapore, Auckland, Sydney and Tokyo, contributing to the global expansion of commercial flight and opening up areas of the world that had previously been accessible only by sea. A trip by boat took weeks, whereas a trip by plane took hours.

In 1951, CPA sent him to Calgary, Alberta, as part of a plan to repair and refurbish crashed and broken-down Royal Canadian Air Force and Royal Canadian Navy aircraft. He was 57 years old, and he had a son who was almost a man, a daughter he adored and a wife he loved as intensely as the day they were married. As he worked, he hummed to himself, and his days were often interrupted by requests from his co-workers to tell stories about the war, about diphtheria and about hunting men from the air. He never complained and never turned anyone down. He knew he had accomplished some extraordinary things in life and did not mind telling others about them.

Perhaps he even knew when it was time to go. Perhaps he knew when he and Denny left to go camping in Utah in June 1952 that he wouldn't be coming back. Maybe he needed to be out in the wild he had helped tame and explore before he could truly be at peace. On June 21, 1952, May waved Denny ahead of him as the two hiked through the Timpanogos Cave National Monument in Utah. May closed his eyes as his left arm tingled, and he grimaced as the pain seared through his chest. He collapsed from another heart attack and died shortly afterwards.

Having spent a lifetime defying the odds, May was not coming back from this trip. In a pocket of his shirt, a note was found with a poem inside it. It was a poem he had written for Vi.

He had already told her about it, already read it to her, but he
needed to keep it with him so that he could believe that on
some level she was always with him.

> *I love you because you are helping me*
> *to make out of the lumber of my life*
> *not a tavern but a temple.*
> *Out of the works of every day,*
> *not a reproach*
> *but a song.*

CHAPTER TWO

~❦~

Clennell Haggerston "Punch" Dickens
1899–1995

JANUARY 29, 1929

The fun part about being a bush pilot, Punch thought to himself, *is that no one problem is exactly like the last one.*

He slapped his mittened hands together against the –40° F cold and tucked them back into the armpits of his rat-skin coat. He watched his breath drift away on the air like cotton as he rounded the tail of his plane to check her whole length for more damage.

Lew Parmenter was also checking the Fokker Super Universal tagged with the ID letters C-GASN. Lew wasn't sure why Punch felt he needed a flight engineer because he knew as much about the engines and component parts of aircraft as any aircraft mechanic. Punch was also widely considered by the boys at Western Canada Airways to be a perfectionist. But here they were, downed near Fort Resolution with a damaged plane in weather so cold that a drop of sweat could freeze on a man's brow before it could fall to the snow.

Punch had been in some pretty bad spots before—he'd been through the Great War—and since then had walked away from more than a few bad situations without a scratch. He always came home. The plane might follow a few days later, but Punch always came back. Such survival was rare these days. Sure, Punch and Wop May, Doc Oaks and dozens of others were storming the North with their planes, trying to pry open Canada's most remote, barren land. Now at almost 30, Punch was among the oldest surviving bush pilots. And he'd only been at it for a few years!

Punch's wife Connie had been at the airport in Edmonton before they'd taken off, and she seemed so nice and pretty. Damned if the two just didn't adore one another. Punch had given her plenty of cause to worry when the newlyweds were stationed in northern Ontario. Once, Punch went missing for two days before a passing plane spotted his signal fire at a lake where he'd ditched because his plane's engine had quit. Another time, Punch had walked through thigh-high snow to get back to her when a storm had forced him down. No matter what chance threw at Punch, he always made it home.

Clennell Haggerston Dickins was born in Portage La Prairie, Manitoba, on January 12, 1899. Unceremoniously tagged with the nickname "Punch" during his childhood, he didn't really know how the nickname had been conceived. His brother Francis claimed to have coined it, but Punch also clearly recalled his Aunt Nell referring to him as a "fat little punch" when he was a small, doughy boy. Not that "Punch" was any worse than "Clennell Haggerston," but the sentiment of being tagged as a fat child was not one he really enjoyed during his teenage years.

Punch's family moved from Manitoba to Edmonton, Alberta, when his father took a job as a bank manager. In 1915, Punch enrolled in the mechanical engineering program at the University of Alberta in Edmonton, but quit the following year

Punch Dickins poses for this photo in 1930. As a bush pilot for Western Canada Airways, Punch always wore this coat while operating in cold weather. The parka was made entirely of rat skins and furs, and though its origins are peculiar, it kept him warm in some of the North's harshest weather.

for the same reason many young Canadian men gave up their educations and careers—the Great War. It was only two years old at the time, and the idea of adventure in faraway Europe seemed attractive, almost romantic, to a young man in Edmonton. Punch joined up with the 196th Western Universities' Battalion of the Canadian Expeditionary Force. He was posted to the infantry but became captivated with those hardy souls who battled in the skies over Europe. As he watched the small specks in the sky swarm one another above the battlefield like an angry nest of hornets, he wished that he was able to do what they did, to feel what they felt.

Shortly after he completed his basic training, Punch transferred to the Royal Flying Corps and was posted to a base in France with renowned Canadian ace Billy Bishop. Over the next six months, Punch flew DH-9 reconnaissance bombers over enemy lines, downed seven enemy aircraft and, at the end of his tour, was awarded the Distinguished Flying Cross, the highest military honor in the flying corps. When he returned home to Edmonton at the age of 19, he was one of the original surviving officers in Canada's fledgling air force, the Canadian Flying Corps.

He made another attempt at school and even played football for the Edmonton Eskimos football club. But he dropped out of school for good in 1921 to return to the air force. He was posted in Alberta, testing parachutes over High River and Siskin fighters in the skies over Edmonton. He worked on fighter engines, trying to find ways to protect them from the intense cold of Canada's North. But important as his work was, Punch always wondered about other uses for aircraft. It occurred to him that using aircraft to deliver mail to remote areas seemed a straightforward solution to a problem, drastically reducing the amount of time it took to deliver a letter. Acting on his idea, he wrote to the headquarters of Canadian Pacific Railways, describing his idea and recommending the company start up an airline to service the North. The letter found its way to the office of James Richardson, grain magnate and owner of the upstart Western Canada Airways (WCA). Intrigued by the young man's idea, Richardson sought out and hired Punch as a pilot for his airline.

That same year, 1927, Punch married Connie, a young graduate of the University of Alberta drama program. He was so smitten with her that he once flew his plane underneath Edmonton's High Level Bridge to impress her, a stunt so dangerous few ever tried it. The stunt worked.

Punch was posted to Western Canada Airways' base in Gold Pines, Ontario, just south of Hudson. He left for Gold Pines a few months before Connie could join him, taking the train to Winnipeg before flying up to the camp. Western Canada Airways had just completed a major government contract, shipping a team of geologists and their supplies to Fort Churchill to build a stretch of railroad between Hudson and Fort Churchill. Next, the company focused on flying mining engineers and prospectors across the Canadian Shield as these determined men unlocked the mineral secrets that lay below its rocky exterior.

But being a rookie pilot with WCA, Punch was due for a little hardship. On his first flight, Punch was scheduled to fly Jack Hammel, president of Howey Mines and one of Western Canada Airways' most important customers, to Red Lake, Ontario. Hammel, however, refused to trust his well-being to a "young bugger who hardly looks dry behind the ears."

Punch didn't so much as flinch or stammer as he replied, "I'm just as eager to get to Red Lake in one piece as you are," he said, tapping his foot impatiently. "Now, get in, and let's go."

"I'll be damned," Hammel muttered to himself, as he watched Dickins turn away and begin walking to the plane. Hammel followed.

Three months later, Connie joined Punch in Gold Pines. He met her in Winnipeg, and Punch flew her into the Gold Pines camp, where the two were given a room in the camp's hotel right above the kitchen. While it was the warmest room in the building, the two could hear all the clamor and noise from the kitchen. From time to time late at night, the cooks broke open a bottle of booze and laughed and talked into the wee hours of the morning. Connie clutched a pillow over her ears, trying to drown out the noise, while Punch laughed himself to sleep.

While living in Gold Pines, Connie began to write in her diary, documenting her life as the wife of one of Canada's first bush pilots. She detailed her husband's routine as well as her own, describing his mishaps and disappearances and how she coped with his long hours away. She later published a small book based on her diary writings entitled *I Married a Bush Pilot*, which stands as a testament to an important era in aviation history.

During his time at Gold Pines, Punch went missing twice while flying. The first time, he was forced down by a blizzard just a few hours after takeoff and walked several miles through thigh-high snow back to camp. The second time, Punch's plane quit several hours out of camp, and he was forced to land on a frozen lake nearby. Unable to repair the plane and not really knowing the lay of the land, Punch set up a camp on the shores of the lake, built a fire with twigs and slept in the plane. He kept busy foraging for wood to keep the fire going and huddling in his plane, trying to stay warm. He endured two nights of bitter cold and loneliness and, on the second night, he began to wonder what he would do if no one came. He had five days of rations that he could stretch a few more days if he was careful, and he could use his rifle to hunt. But with little idea of where he was, he didn't even know which way to start walking.

Early on the third day, as Punch chewed on tinned fruit, he heard a roar suddenly break over the lake and saw a plane flash overhead. Punch shot to his feet, spilling his breakfast as he jumped up and down, flapping his arms. The plane waggled its wings from side to side, banked left and then lined up for a landing. The pilot had seen the smoke from Punch's fire and swooped down immediately to rescue him. When the plane landed at Gold Pines and Punch exited the plane, Connie was waiting. She threw her arms around him, and she didn't let go for several minutes.

By August 1928, Western Canada Airways and some of its competitors were slowly prying open Canada's most secluded and remote geography. But most of the northern parts of the country were still unexplored and unmapped. Few maps of the Yukon and Northwest Territories existed, and those were less than accurate. Punch would change all of that with a little help from the "Colonel."

It was September 1928, and Punch had been contracted by Colonel Robert MacAlpine of Dominion Explorers to check on several of his bases along the coastline of Hudson Bay and the interior of the Northwest Territories. If all went as planned, they would cover 4000 miles in less than 12 days.

It was destined to be tricky. The endurance of Punch's Fokker G-CASK depended on caches of fuel stored at strategic locations. And for one stretch, the one over the Barren Lands of the Northwest Territories, there would be no cache. No reliable mapping of the Barren Lands had been done, so most maps of the area simply identified the area as "Unexplored." Many people had tried to make the trip across the region on foot or sled, but their stories usually ended in starvation, even cannibalism. The Barren Lands were empty, with nary a bush or animal—just 400 miles of rock and tundra. Punch shuddered inwardly at the thought of crashing there. They'd be doomed.

Departing Winnipeg on August 30, they followed the Nelson River and reached Fort Churchill by August 31. As they soared in to land, Punch looked out the window and saw pods of whales breaching the surface of Hudson Bay. Richard Pearce, editor of the *Northern Miner*, who was along to write about the trip, pressed his nose against the glass and smiled. He'd never seen whales before.

They put down at Baker Lake for fuel on September 1, and the next morning, all three men rose feeling unsettled. Ahead, under a crystal sky, lay the unmapped expanse of the Barren Lands. Punch soared into the air and brought the plane to a southwesterly heading. The word "unexplored" flashed in his brain, and he tried to lighten his mood by pondering who among their party would taste the most delicious in the event they crashed.

Trees became sparser below them until they could see none at all. The sun gleamed off standing pools of water, small lakes and ribbons of streams that cut the rock into smaller and smaller portions. Not a single hill rose from the land, only jagged outcroppings of rock. Punch had heard of the deserts in Africa that were miles of endless sand, where no bush or animal could live under the blazing hot sun. In Canada's North, the land was just as inhospitable, even in September. He felt a sense of hopelessness just looking at it.

For the first hour, Punch's plan to navigate the Barren Lands worked. Knowing the position of major bodies of water, such as Baker Lake behind him, Lake Athabasca to the southwest and the Dubawnt River and other, smaller rivers in between, Punch kept his eyes firmly fixed on his instruments, making minute adjustments to the control column to keep the plane on course. But slowly the rivers and streams began to fall away until nothing but gray emptiness stared up at him. The sky and land seemed to meld at the horizon until it was difficult to distinguish sky from ground. He felt his brain begin to whisper that he was headed the wrong way, that he was too far south and needed to come north to compensate. Punch responded by believing his instruments. He fixed the bearing of the sun in relation to the plane and time of day and decided he was actually headed in the right direction. The horizon could lie, but the sun could not.

The whispers went away.

"I haven't seen a single goddamn living thing out there this whole time," the Colonel said.

Pearce scribbled furiously in his notebook, stopping only to whittle a new lead for his pencil with his pocketknife.

"Not true," Punch responded, pointing out the left window. A single seagull circled lazily below.

"That poor bugger's gonna starve to death out here," the Colonel harrumphed.

"Only thing out here to break the wind are some poor, lonely caribou," Pearce chimed in.

The Colonel chuckled and fell silent.

After another hour, something flashed up ahead. Punch checked his map, then his bearings and descended for a closer look at the glassy pool ahead. He breathed a sigh of relief as the outline of Lake Dubawnt took shape, then reached back to shake the Colonel's leg in relief. The lake below signaled the end of the worst of the Barren Lands. Punch brought the SK farther south until he was flying directly over the river. In another hour, the vegetation returned, and they saw a herd of caribou grazing below. All three sighed audibly. They had survived the Barren Lands, and no one had been forced to become dinner.

They put down that night at Stony Rapids on the Cat River where the local RCMP contingent put them up. While the residents offered hospitality easily, the fort's commander didn't want to deplete their fuel cache. He argued with Punch that he simply had no fuel to give. But the Colonel excused Punch and Pearce from the room, and when he returned a half-hour later, the RCMP commander ordered SK gassed up.

From the moment they left the ground, they fought the northern winds, and Punch's heart sank with the fuel gauge as it dipped lower and lower towards the large "E" at the bottom. At a quarter of a tank, the needle steadied and didn't move. Punch thought they might make it, but soon the engine began to sputter and finally it quit altogether. The fuel gauge had obviously frozen, and regardless of what it said, the engine wasn't running.

Everyone tightened their harnesses and held on to something sturdy as Punch lined SK up with the Slave River below. He looked as far ahead of the plane as he could, watching for rocks or sandbanks or even a moose the plane might hit on landing. Punch's eagle eyes marked a spot of blue several hundred feet ahead, devoid of any shadow or animal, and he lowered the plane until the floats kissed the water. A gentle sinking sensation announced their arrival.

Punch pointed the plane at the banks of the river and managed to beach it close to shore. The three men quickly jumped out of the plane in order to secure it to several stout trees with rope. Once they were sure that the plane wasn't going anywhere, they sat down on some nearby rocks to discuss what they were going to do.

"May as well start a fire," Punch broke silence, heading back to the plane. "Anyone want some tea?

Over steaming mugs of tea, the three outlined their options. They were about 60 miles from Fort Smith, a good hike through unknown territory with few supplies. And who knows what might become of the plane during their absence. No one knew where they were, so staying with the plane offered no better chance of survival. Punch looked around at the foliage surrounding them and remembered he had an ax in the plane along with the rope. He suggested they build a raft to float the plane down the river. The rest agreed.

Colonel MacAlpine and Pearce headed for the trees to mark prospective logs and branches for the raft while Punch headed for the plane to fetch the rope, ax and knives. He hopped from rock to rock, then gracefully leaped onto the float of SK and took a moment to steady himself. That's when he heard it.

It was a gentle coughing that sounded above the burble of the river, tickled his ears, suggesting that something was out there. Punch stood motionless, holding his breath. The coughing slowly grew louder, but Punch still hadn't the faintest idea what he was hearing.

Then a cry not found in nature sounded over the water, and Punch shook his head in amazement. Again the whistle sounded, and Punch scrambled into the plane to fish for his field glasses. He scurried to the front of the plane and trained the glasses downstream. It took his eyes a moment to focus, and it took his mind another to believe what he was seeing. Beneath a cloud of black smoke, a steamboat was chugging right towards them.

"Well, I'll be!" Punch bellowed in joy.

He leaped out of the plane, lost his footing and tumbled into the icy waters of the Slave River. He sprang to his feet, splashed back to shore and tore up the river as fast as he could, sprinting towards the steamer. He stumbled, tripping over rocks and roots, and he fell to the ground more than once only to shoot right back to his feet. When he was even with the steamer, he began hollering, waving and jumping up and down. For a frightening moment, no one on the steamer acknowledged him. But then a series of blasts on its whistle erupted, and the ship began to turn towards the shore.

"I don't believe it," Pearce whispered, as Punch bolted past where he and the Colonel were piling wood on a rocky quay that jutted out into the river. Punch stood as far out as he could in the river, waiting for the ship to come close. The steamer slowed as it neared the plane, then slipped anchor and crawled to a halt.

An enormous man in a lumberjack shirt and a Stetson stepped onto the deck of the ship.

"Ahoy!" he shouted. "Are you fellows in trouble?"

Punch laughed. "Not exactly!" he shouted back. "But would you happen to have any airplane gasoline on that barge?"

Silence. Punch strained his ears for a response but heard nothing. He was just about to ask again when the most impossible answer reached his ears.

"Yes," the man replied, his voice betraying his bewilderment. "There are 10 barrels for some chap named Dickins who thinks he is going to fly in here next winter."

Punch was so shocked that he lost his footing and almost fell into the river again.

"I'll take that off your hands then!" he shouted back. "I'm Dickins!"

"Well I'll be damned," the Colonel whispered under his breath.

Pearce didn't look up. He'd gotten out his notebook again and continued writing.

It turned out that Punch's bosses at WCA had decided to set up a fuel cache along the banks of the river for his future use. The timing was, everyone agreed, uncanny. Within hours, Punch had his plane fueled and, with a dip of his wings in salute to the intrepid steamer, Punch and his passengers took to the skies heading for Fort Smith. The rest of the flight was uneventful, and one year later, Punch was awarded the McKee Trophy for his pioneering flight across the Barren Lands.

But there was other work to be done. Western Canada Airways, still itching to prove to the government the feasibility of delivering mail by air, began flying an airmail route from Edmonton to Regina in November 1928. Punch piloted the inaugural flight, but because the government still didn't believe

Punch Dickins (second from right) delivers the first load of airmail to Cameron Bay, NWT, in 1932.

the idea was feasible, and the mail was strictly a government responsibility, WCA terminated the venture only two months later. Undaunted, on January 22, 1929, Punch took off from Fort McMurray in –50° F weather with a planeload of mail, bound for Aklavik, Yukon Territory, on Canada's most northern shore of the Arctic Ocean. Punch, in the company of postal inspector T.J. O'Reilly and engineer Lew Parmenter, would deliver the mail to Aklavik and all points in between to prove the utility of delivering mail by air.

Six days after leaving Edmonton, Punch and his passengers reached Fort Resolution, just south of Fort Smith. Punch swung the plane around nearby Great Slave Lake and lined up for a landing on its frozen surface. At first the landing area seemed perfectly flat. But Punch missed a snow-covered ice hummock, and the plane hit the large bump at high speed, sending it nose first into the ground. Recoiling and spinning wildly with metal groaning, the plane took on an unnatural list to the left. When it finally came to a halt, Punch tore off his seatbelt and ran out to the front of the plane to examine the damage. His heart sank. Both blades of the propeller were mangled, and the undercarriage that connected the left ski to the plane was damaged. With no spare parts handy and the closest telegraph office six days away by dog team, Punch and his passengers faced the unappealing prospect of staying four to six months at Fort Resolution until spare parts could be shipped in by boat. In his usual unassuming way, Punch proposed to Lew that the two of them simply try to *fix* the damaged plane.

"I don't relish the thought of spending six months this far north," Punch said.

They propped up the plane on gas cans and constructed a makeshift shelter for the nose out of stout poles and animal skins, then retired for the night.

But Punch had problems sleeping and eventually gave up. Instead, he pulled on his furs and mittens and ventured back outside towards the plane. The surrounding land, obscured by cloud and snow, seemed as black as anything Punch had seen in his life, and he sighed loudly.

"Times of despair," a voice sounded behind him, "are designed to test our faith."

Punch turned and saw the priest of the fort's Catholic mission standing beside him. Punch remembered him helping with the plane the night before but hadn't learned his name.

"You're up early, Father," Punch responded softly.

"I am always awake before the sun rises to pray and give thanks to God," the priest said.

"Thanks?" Punch asked sardonically.

"Indeed," the holy man replied. "I have been chosen by the Lord to spread the word of our Savior across this great land. I have been sent to bring His love and peace to those who do not yet believe."

He turned to Punch, his face solemn. "You have also been chosen to do His work. You have been given the skill and the blessing to open up these lands with your machine. You will help unite this nation. You will bring happiness to many more people than you can imagine."

Punch avoided the priest's eyes. He felt embarrassed for reasons he couldn't understand.

"As for your plane, I wouldn't worry," the priest said, fumbling in his robes. "As I said, you have the skill and blessing of the Lord, and He does work through us to help one another." With that, the priest pulled from his robe a three-foot-long piece of water pipe. Punch gasped. It was the perfect length and circumference needed to repair the undercarriage.

"Father, thank you so much," he gushed, grasping the pipe. The priest laughed.

"In whatever way you choose to have it, my son, do have some faith." He turned and shuffled back to the fort saying, "Difficult times such as these can be trying, but the solution is often a matter of faith."

The next day Punch and Lew began hammering out the mangled propeller. They were able to straighten the first blade without incident, but the second snapped off in Punch's hand, effectively stranding them at Fort Resolution.

After shouting curses across the lake, Punch stormed into the fort and hired a Slavey and his dog team to take a message to Fort Smith, asking that a telegram be sent to Edmonton ordering the necessary parts. Fort Smith was the closest fort with a telegraph station, still six nights by dog team. Even on receipt of the message, no one knew when the part would arrive. Days if a plane and part were available, weeks or months if sent by dog team.

Punch slept poorly that night. He lay on his cot and held a photo of himself and Connie in front of his face, even though he could not see it in the deep darkness of the northern night. He loved her, and he knew he'd given her cause to worry more than a few times. But she knew the risks of his job as well as he and had heard stories of some pilot disappearing or another one crashing. Punch wondered if his luck would run out some day.

He rolled over and fell asleep.

In the morning he awoke with purpose and found that the room empty. He slipped on his moccasins and strode to the kitchen of the mission, where he found Lew drinking tea by the fire.

"You know, I've got a hacksaw with my tools," Punch stated before the door had even closed behind him. "Suppose we file down the broke side of the prop, then take nine inches off the good side to even it out. Do you think the ruddy plane would fly?"

Lew didn't respond. He grabbed his coat and walked out the door.

They were careful, using small, measured strokes, not pulling too hard. They shaped the broken blade to a tip, then got to work on the other side. Slowly and deliberately, they took their time making all the cuts. Hours passed, but just after noon, their stomachs growling from not having eaten all day and their toes tingling from the cold, they shaved off the last inch of aluminum and stood back.

"What do you think?" Punch asked Lew.

"I think you should take it for a spin," Lew responded.

"You coming?" Punch asked, making for the plane.

Lew shook his head. "Someone has to tell Connie what happened to you."

Seated in the plane, Punch gave the thumbs-up, and Lew spun the prop. Punch pushed the ignition, opened the throttles and the plane roared to life. He let her warm up for a few minutes then turned the plane into the wind and checked his instruments.

Now or never, Lord, Punch thought, recalling the priest's words. Taking a deep breath, he opened the throttles wide and released the brakes. At first, it didn't look good. The shortened prop didn't generate the same power, and he felt as if he was taxiing slower than usual. But the lake was large, and Punch had plenty of room for takeoff. With the wind flowing underneath his wings, he soon felt the plane skip off the ground. He closed his eyes, hauled back on the control stick and felt the plane soar into the air. Within a week, Punch and his party were back in Edmonton. Six months later, Punch finally made the trip to Aklavik, stunning the Inuit who had never before seen a machine that could fly.

In the course of all his flying throughout the Northwest Territories, Punch had noticed a pinkish hue along the shores of Great Bear Lake, standing out from the surrounding tundra.

Punch Dickins, taken in 1930

On one occasion, while carrying geologist Gilbert Labine, Punch pointed out the blossoms of pink and orange and asked what they were. Labine ordered Punch to descend for a closer look, and when he looked up, Labine wore a smile that covered his whole face.

"This is elephant country," Labine whispered. He explained to Punch that the pinkish hues were cobalt blooms, signs of radium and uranium, which were exceedingly rare minerals. By 1936, Great Bear Lake had become the largest uranium mine in the world. The uranium that fueled the atom bomb dropped on Hiroshima in August 1945, ending the Second World War, came from the mine that Punch helped to discover.

Satisfied with Punch's demonstration of the use of the airplane to deliver mail, the Canadian government finally offered Western Canada Airways a contract to establish the Prairie Air Mail Service in January 1930. Punch made the inaugural flight on March 3 from Regina to Edmonton and continued to fly routes that later included Winnipeg, Moose Jaw, Medicine Hat and Calgary.

In November of the same year, Western Canada Airways was bought out by Canadian Airways. Rather than clean house, the new company elected to retain most of WCA's staff, including Punch. They even promoted him, making him Superintendent of the Mackenzie District and then Superintendent of Northern Operations. Punch was responsible for coordinating the efforts of more than 20 planes and 50 men, and he reveled in the responsibility. His precise, perfectionist nature made him the perfect planner, and Canadian Airways managed to hold its own in a business climate that was becoming increasingly turbulent.

By 1932, Canada was deep in the throes of the Great Depression. The crash of the stock market and a searing drought across the Prairies caused record unemployment. Thousands of Canadians were without jobs, lining up for hours at a time to interview for a single opening. As a result, the Canadian government was more concerned with its national fiscal situation and alleviating the effects of the depression than with the prompt delivery of mail, so it canceled Canadian Airways' contract in 1932.

That didn't stop Punch from flying. From July 16 to August 16, 1935, Punch flew for almost an entire month throughout the Canadian North. He flew Dr. Charles Camsell, Deputy Minister of Mines and Resources, on a study of northern mines and field parties. He then picked up Don Maclean, Superintendent of Airways and Airports for the Department of Defence, to investigate the establishment of a northern airway system. Along the way, Punch and engineer Bill Sunderland photographed much of the Yukon and NWT for mapping. In all, Punch flew 8400 miles in just over 81 hours that summer. For that feat, his pioneering of delivery of mail by air and his precedent-setting flight over the Barren Lands in 1928, Punch sailed for England where, in the royal halls of Buckingham Palace, home of the British Monarchy, he was named an Officer of the Order of the British Empire.

In 1939, war broke out in Europe. Adolf Hitler, at the head of the Nazi Party of Germany, began biting off chunks of Europe. Flaunting the conditions of the Treaty of Versailles, Hitler built an enormous war machine and proceeded to annex Austria and Czechoslovakia. When the Wehrmacht stepped over the sovereign boundary of Poland, the world responded as Canada and Britain both declared war on Germany. After the invasion of Poland, Prime Minister Mackenzie-King dispatched a message to the Prime Minister of Great Britain, asking for clarification as to what declaring war entailed...exactly.

Allied forces retreated to the isolated safety of Great Britain and began pounding German strongholds from the air. Using vast formations of bomber aircraft, the Allies unleashed an aerial bombardment on Europe that far outstripped the pitiful tonnage of explosives that had been dropped in all of World War I. Allied bombers targeted factories, power plants, shipyards and military formations. A combination of incendiary and high explosive bombs dropped on the German city of

Dresden ignited a firestorm that killed over 100,000 men, women and children in February 1945.

Punch put his managerial and planning skills to work for the war effort. In 1941, the Canadian Pacific Railway Company (Air Services) hired Dickins to manage the delivery of Canadian and American combat aircraft across the Atlantic to aid in the war effort. The bombing campaign against Germany was proving effective but costly because the Nazis shot down so many aircraft every day. Under Dickins' management, reserve pilots from Canada and the U.S. ferried fighters and bombers overseas to keep the Allied air forces equipped. At the end of the war, to Punch's horror, he realized he had managed his assignment so well that his department had actually turned a profit of over $1 million from the contract. Punch quickly issued a check to Ottawa for the difference.

Following the war, Punch was snapped up as sales director for the deHavilland Aircraft Company of Canada in 1947. His key task was to develop the ultimate bush plane. Until this time, bush planes were often little more than surplus war aircraft or small passenger planes. Few were designed to withstand the rigors of Canada's North.

But instead of relying on his own experience, Punch contacted dozens of existing bush pilots to ask them what they would like to see in a bush plane. From the input he received, Punch helped design and build the deHavilland Beaver, an aircraft that became known as one of the true workhorses of the North. Its rugged construction, high wings and powerful engine gave bush pilots one of the most reliable aircraft ever built. It was even voted one of the 10 most important Canadian engineering feats of the 20th century.

In 1957, Punch exceeded the standard set by the Beaver when he helped deHavilland design the Twin Otter. Used as a passenger plane, cargo plane, bush plane and water bomber,

Punch Dickins, Frank McDougall, T.M. Reid, A.F. McDonald, P.C. Garrat inspect the prototype of the deHavilland Beaver, 1947.

~ఌ⫯ఌ~

the Twin Otter was used into the 21st century as the plane of choice for many northern pilots.

Although he retired in 1966, the honors and awards did not stop for Punch Dickins. In 1967, he was made a fellow of the Canadian Aeronautics and Space Institute. And in 1973, he was inducted as an Officer of the Order of Canada and named to Canada's Aviation Hall of Fame. He was selected as the Hall's first president and director, and in the later years of his life, continued to contribute to the growth of aviation in Canada.

When Punch Dickins surrendered his pilot's license at the age of 77, it wasn't because he needed to. His eyesight was perfect, his reflexes quick and his mind sharp and practiced. But Punch was starting to wind down, preferring instead to dote on his grandchildren and enjoy his golden years. But slowly, almost imperceptibly at first, Punch began to withdraw from the world around him. He began speaking less and less, stopped going outside and even, in the last few months before his death, stopped talking to Connie, his beloved wife of almost 70 years. At 96, Punch was a living legend in Canada's aviation community and was named by *Macleans* magazine as one of the 100 most influential Canadians of the 20th century.

He had done so much in his life, and now it was time to go. When he breathed his last breath in Toronto in August 1995, Connie was beside him. Four years later, at the age of 99, Connie also passed away. Her obituary in the *Edmonton Journal* was a testimony not only to her life, but to Punch's as well:

Connie and Punch
To new frontiers, together forever.

CHAPTER THREE

Harold A. "Doc" Oaks

1896–1968

IN CANADA'S BLEAK NORTH, time seemed to disappear. Day blended into night, night into day, with no way to mark the passing of each hour. In the summertime, the days stretched into eternity, and the sun never set; in the winter, it never rose. Perpetual light and perpetual darkness, bone-chilling cold, freezing winds, and worst of all, solitude—bare mind-numbing solitude that could drive the hardiest of men insane.

The prospector couldn't remember when he'd been dropped off. He didn't even know what day it was or what month it was. His sole preoccupation was with staying warm and finding food, so deep it was in the Canadian winter that almost nothing moved. But the lure of gold was stronger than the will and common sense of most men, so he'd sold his land back in Manitoba and journeyed North to stake his claim and make his fortune in sweet yellow gold.

Some days it was too cold and too windy to leave his tent, and he would sit, wrapped in furs and blankets, singing to himself against the roar of the wind. When the blizzards faded, he crawled out of the tent, pan in hand, and began to work the nearby riverbed, searching for the slightest glimmer of a bright, rich future. His hair was long and grimy, his beard thick and matted; he couldn't remember the last time he had bathed.

But he was running low on supplies, even bullets to hunt game. He was down to his last few rations, his clothes hadn't been washed since the summer and he hadn't tasted the sweet smoke of tobacco in months. Several weeks ago, slowly realizing his situation was getting worse with each passing day, he had constructed a giant arrow on the ground from tree branches, hoping that *he* would see them.

One day, the prospector was parked at the side of the creek, working the grit and slime of the river through the fine sieve of his gold pan, when a giant roar split the late afternoon air. He looked up, terrified, and saw a large-winged shadow pass over him. The shadow flew lower and lower until it became a machine with wings. It bounced several times as its skis hit the ground a few hundred yards away, and the prospector yelped with glee and ran towards the plane, churning snow beneath his feet. He tripped just as he reached the airplane and fell into the arms of a short, wiry, mustached man who dropped down out of the cockpit.

"What day is it?" he screamed at the aviator, grabbing him by the front of his jacket as the prospector's starved psyche blitzed the newcomer for information. "What month is it? What news do you bring? Do you have any tobacco?"

The man in the helmet and goggles laughed and gently pulled the prospector's hands away from the lapels of his coat.

"It's Friday, it's February and yes, I have tobacco," the man smiled, trying not to breathe through his nose lest the ripe smell of the grimy prospector overwhelm him. He turned to reach into the cockpit of the plane for supplies, but the wild-eyed, bushy-bearded prospector stopped him.

"It's you," he whispered in amazement. "It's really you. You're him. You're 'Doc!'"

The pilot's face fell at the nickname. He opened his mouth to respond, closed it, then opened it again.

"Yes," he sighed in resignation. "I am 'Doc.' But please don't call me that."

◈

Born in Hespeler, Ontario, on November 12, 1896, Harold Oaks had never left Ontario before he enlisted in the Canadian Corps in 1915. His education had been in the public school system in Hespeler and Preston, and he was raised in a relatively affluent home. His father was a doctor, and because Harold mirrored his father so much in mentality and mannerism, he had gone almost his entire life by the nickname "Doc." It followed him everywhere he went. Someone always figured it out, no matter how many times he asked people not to call him by that name. It followed him through a year at the University of Toronto as he took an economics course in the Faculty of Arts. When he joined the Royal Canadian Corps as a signal rider and was sent overseas in 1916, it didn't take long for his fellow soldiers to also tag him with that most hated nickname. Even when he was posted to the Canadian contingent engaged in the Battle of the Somme, the war-weary troops still summoned him by the name "Doc." At first he protested, but he soon learned to ignore it.

The Somme was hell, and Oaks was deep inside. The crack of rifles split the air around him, and the crash and bang of shell after shell hammered at his sanity. All around the young motorcycle dispatch rider, stretchers filled the trenches, holding the wounded and the dead. Some of the wounded screamed in pain, while others lay silently, the rise and fall of their chests the only sign that they were still alive. The mud of the French countryside soaked up the blood from open wounds as it had already soaked up the lives of countless soldiers.

He had not been in the Somme an entire day, and already some of his comrades-in-arms recognized him as Doc. At first he protested, imploring his new friends to call him Harold, but his pleas fell on deaf ears and on minds weary from the day-to-day struggle of war.

Convinced that antiquated army tactics would overcome the endless defensive line of trenches that snaked through France and Belgium, General Douglas Haig had planned a massive offensive along the stretch of the Somme River in France, between Albert and Arras. The plan called for an eight-day bombardment of the German trenches to annihilate their concrete bunkers and barbed wire, followed by a huge assault of 750,000 British and French troops with cavalry held in reserve to exploit any progress.

But in February 1916, the Germans assaulted the French stronghold of Verdun, and the Somme offensive was quickly implemented as a diversionary tactic to relieve the besieged French troops. On July 1, the bombardment began, and the Germans, already wise to the Allied forces' intent, merely holed up in their trenches until the shelling ceased. When the first British troops surged into no-man's-land, they were raked with intense defensive fire. Those that made it past no-man's-land found bunkers and barbed wire still intact. On the first day of battle, the British Expeditionary Force suffered 58,000 casualties, almost one-third of its strength.

When the attack bogged down in August, the Canadian Corps was committed to the battle, including the Signal Corps to which 20-year-old Harold Oaks belonged. It was his first day, and he was already sick of it, ready to go home. He had already seen men shot or vaporized by enemy artillery. He did not know how he was going to survive the war.

He was making his way back to his unit through the miles and miles of trenches when he turned a corner and ran smack into an enormous, dirty man.

"What's this?" the man in a Canadian uniform roared at the dispatch rider. "Can't you see where you're going?"

"Sorry about that," Doc responded. "Still learning my way around, ya know."

"I'll learn ya," the larger man responded, pushing the sleeves of his uniform above his elbows. "I'll teach ya to watch where you're going!"

Men began to crowd around the pair as the large, dirty man squared off with Doc. Doc stared him down, not making a fist or any sort of move. A third man jumped in from the midst of the gathering soldiers. His name was Clark Ruse.

"Johnson!" Ruse barked at the larger man. "Lay off him!"

"Stay out of it," Doc grumbled. "I can handle myself."

The growing horde gasped collectively at his brashness then grew silent. Johnson paused in shock, and with a frustrated wipe of his hand and a growl, he turned and began to push his way through the gathered crowd. Oaks watched the behemoth go, fear gluing him to where he stood. His fellow soldiers clapped him on the back.

Doc survived the Somme as a dispatch rider, and in 1917, just after the Battle of Vimy Ridge, was transferred to the Royal Flying Corps (RFC) to learn to be a fighter pilot. He had put in the request because he was entranced with the aerial spectacle that these vaunted knights of the sky put on day after day. It was dangerous work, and the airplanes themselves were unreliable. Still, Oaks committed himself to his new vocation, learning to fly Maurice Forman Shorthorns, B.E.s and Bristol Fighters. He learned the basics of flight, combat, reconnaissance and gunnery, and in March 1918, he was posted back to France with the 48th Squadron of the RFC. Just two months later, he was commissioned a Captain, having racked up 11 kills before war's end. He was even awarded a Distinguished Flying Cross for his bravery and skill. He loved flying more than combat, and while on patrol, would often stare out over the wide expanse of the French countryside. He considered the swaths of forest, farmlands and miles of mud, and the utility of the airplane began to increasingly inspire him. An idea began to form, fleetingly at first and quickly discarded when combat ensued. But when he returned to Canada in May 1919, he took a summer mining course at Queen's University in Kingston, Ontario, and his plan began to coalesce. If the airplane could be used to locate enemy positions, surely it could be used to locate minerals in some of Canada's most isolated places.

Following his stint at Queen's, Oaks enrolled in the mining engineering course at the University of Toronto. He worked hard in class and even harder in the field during the summertime. In 1920, he spent his summer at Kirkland Lake at the Tec Hughes Gold Mine. In 1921, he was an assistant geologist in Fort Norman, Northwest Territories, and in 1922, signed on with the Geological Survey of Canada in Michipicoten, Ontario. When the time came to plan his thesis project for his fourth year, he approached his supervising professor and asked for special permission to do his thesis on a non-mining subject—"an investigation of the advantages of thick wing sections in commercial aircraft"—under the supervision of the Department of Mechanical Engineering. Doc explained his plan to Professor H.E.T. Haultain and laid out his vision for the use of the airplane in mineral exploration. He pointed out that the university even had a wind tunnel he could use.

"I think it's different, and it might work," Haultain concluded. "I expect you to keep me apprised of your progress."

Oaks successfully completed his thesis and, upon graduation, began to look for work in the mining industry, hoping to find a company open to his idea of linking mining and flight. After a brief stint with Hollinger Gold Mines searching for minerals in Northern Ontario and Quebec, Doc jumped at the chance to become a pilot for the Ontario Provincial Air Service (OPAS) in July 1924. After taking a refresher flying course,

Oaks took to the skies on forest fire patrol, spending endless hours flying predictable patterns over Ontario's forests. Flying one of the OPAS' gigantic U.S. surplus HS2L Flying Boats, Oaks logged hundreds of flight hours, keeping his eyes peeled for smoke and fire. He picked up on the growing migration throughout the area of Red Lake as word of gold began to reach the ears of enterprising men. Another gold rush was beginning in Canada, this time at Red Lake. Men from all over North America converged on the area in the hope of finding their fortune in gold.

Oaks heard of it as well and mentally struggled every day he spent aloft with the idea of heading into the bush and staking a claim of his own. The chances of making it rich were small, Oaks told himself, and the day-to-day existence of a prospector was less than glamorous. But when his supervisor Tommy Thompson suggested they go for it, Oaks agreed immediately. It was the validation Oaks was looking for and, within a week of their decision, the two quit their jobs and were mushing their way by dogsled towards Northern Ontario and their chance at a fortune in gold.

They were lucky. With Doc's training and Thompson's woodland skills, they were able to mark several claims that proved profitable for several months. By day, Oaks and Thompson panned for gold along Red Lake. When night came and Oaks folded himself in his sleeping bag and listened to the silence of the land around him, he thought about the plains of France and his thesis. He wondered if he could someday realize his vision of mining and flight.

From time to time, he and Tommy came across other prospectors who had joined the gold rush and were desperately starved for human contact. Some begged for provisions, tobacco, soap and even food. The life of the prospector was solitary, and more and more, Oaks began to see an opportunity for himself. When Thompson eventually voiced his wish

Doc Oaks with his Curtiss Lark of Patricia Airways Explorations in 1926

to return to civilization, Oaks implemented his plan to go into business.

After Thompson returned to the OPAS, Oaks sold his stake for a share in an upstart freight company called Patricia Airways and Exploration Ltd. As a pilot for Patricia Airways, Oaks flew the company's single Curtiss Lark biplane, shipping prospectors and supplies from Sioux Lookout in Ontario throughout

the Red Lake and Woman Lake areas. In just over a year of flying on both skis and floats in all kinds of weather to all kinds
of places, Oaks carried some 260 passengers and 140,000
pounds of freight for hopeful prospectors. Patricia Airways
even began to charge 25 cents to transport a letter by air, proving the viability of airmail. Without government subsidy, Oaks
and Patricia Airways hauled over 3000 pounds of mail.

Oaks soon became well known to the prospectors who
had charged north to Red Lake to find their fortune. He took
them tobacco, food, ammunition and other supplies and
often randomly landed at campsites just to check in and see
how things were. On more than one occasion, stir-crazy,
unwashed, and unshaven men burst from their tents towards
the slight, mustached pilot, demanding to know the date,
the month, the year and asking for news and extra provisions.
Although he swore he never told a soul about his hated nickname, many of those he served, whom he had never met
before, knew him as Doc, the man who swooped down from
the skies to bring them not only the staples of existence, but
human contact as well.

On one occasion, a rather enterprising gold seeker asked
Oaks to bring him a sack of oats for his horse. Oaks had flown
in supplies to several other men in the area, landing on a small,
icy lake. This particular man had thought it more efficient to
use a horse to carry his supplies—and even himself—but was
now faced with the challenge of feeding it.

"How much will it be for 100 pounds of oats?" the man
inquired while Oaks unloaded other supplies for other clients.

"We charge a dollar a pound for freight," Oaks responded
with a smirk on his face.

"What?" the prospector with the horse exploded. "That's
highway robbery!"

"That's the price of business," Oaks shrugged. The grizzled
man grudgingly conceded, and Doc hopped back in his plane

to take off. But while taxiing for takeoff, the ice beneath the plane cracked and one ski became lodged in the ice. Oaks was forced to ask the man and his horse to help free his plane. When Oaks returned some days later with the bag of oats, he asked the man for his payment.

"Why, I believe the cost of the tow should cover the cost of shipping the oats," the man responded with a wide smile.

"What?" Oaks thundered. "That's highway robbery!"

"That's the price of business," the man smirked, then snickered at his horse and led it away, leaving Oaks fuming beside his plane.

Oaks realized that his plan to provide air service to the mining crews in Red Lake was not profitable work. The number of passengers or amount of freight to be hauled could vary from month to month and even week to week. Tired of working with a company who operated on a shoestring budget in such a small area, Oaks abandoned Patricia Airways for a bigger and better idea.

The idea had come during a chance encounter in Toronto with former Controller of Civil Aviation John Wilson. Oaks was in Toronto to raise money for another plane for Patricia Airways, and Wilson suggested that he talk to James A. Richardson. Richardson was a well-known supporter of the aviation industry and was adventurous in his business pursuits as well as a wealthy industrialist and grain broker in Winnipeg.

"If there's anyone with the money and lack of sense to spring for your idea, it's him," Wilson told Oaks, tipping his hat in farewell.

In 1926, Oaks hopped the train from Toronto to Winnipeg and headed straight to the Winnipeg Grain Exchange. It was a little past 11:00 AM when he strode through the front door and approached the receptionist working the front desk.

"Could you please call Mr. Richardson to the lobby?" Oaks asked the receptionist politely.

"I believe he's on the floor of the exchange at the moment," the man responded. "If you're willing to wait, he should be done soon. It's almost lunchtime."

"I'm sorry, could you please page him now? " Oaks insisted. "It's urgent."

"And you are—?" the receptionist asked, reaching for the microphone.

"Harold Oaks," Oaks responded. "Thank you."

It took only minutes for Richardson to appear in the lobby from the floor of the grain exchange. He wore a quizzical look and a sly smile. He spoke briefly to the receptionist, then made his way towards Oaks.

"Mr. Oaks? Have we met?" Richardson asked, extending his hand.

"We haven't, sir, but I have an idea for an airfreight company that I think you're going to love," Oaks responded, taking his hand. But Richardson looked up and to the left, as if searching his mind for something.

"Oaks…Oaks…Oaks….It's familiar," Richardson mused. Then the light of recognition shone in his eyes. "Oaks! Doc Oaks from Patricia Airways!"

Oaks stared at Richardson with a mix of amazement and consternation, flabbergasted at the mention of his moniker by a man he had never met, but he said nothing.

"I've heard of the work you and Patricia Airways have done out of Sioux Lookout. A most impressive and bold undertaking." Richardson's chest puffed. "I admire that."

"Then, Mr. Richardson, I think you're going to love what I have to tell you," Oaks responded.

Over lunch at a nearby Winnipeg restaurant, Richardson and Oaks formulated their idea for a larger version of Patricia Airways. It wouldn't be just for mining, but for airfreight all across the west, maybe even across the country. Oaks told Richardson of the legions of veteran war pilots who were itching to fly again, and about the potential of the airplane to open up some of the most isolated parts of Canada to the rest of the world. The ability to move men and supplies quickly to snowed-in or remote regions of the country was an undertaking that could make history and a profit as well.

Richardson listened intently as Oaks laid out his vision. He was struck not only by Oaks' enthusiasm for aviation, but for his thoughtful analysis and business sense. When Oaks finished outlining his ideas, Richardson reached into his attaché case for paper and a pen. There, in a Winnipeg restaurant, Western Canada Airways, a new airfreight and transport company was born.

Western Canada Airways began operation in November 1926. Oaks traveled to New York to fly back the company's first plane, a brand-new Fokker Super Universal, a strangely designed airplane with an enclosed cabin for passengers and freight and an open cockpit for the pilot. For his first job, Oaks received a telegram from a businessman in New York who needed a prospector operating in northern Ontario to sign some papers. Oaks flew to a lake near the prospector's camp, snowshoed into the woods and found the prospector, snowshoed back to the plane with him and flew to nearby Sioux Lookout, Ontario. The prospector signed the papers at the bank, and Doc flew him back to his claim deep in the bush of Ontario. What would normally have taken a week or two had been accomplished in a mere afternoon.

Western Canada Airways began to slowly fill a niche in Canada, flying passengers, freight and mail to remote outposts in Manitoba and Ontario. They also began to do aerial mapping, forest surveying and aerial photography. In response to the increased demand, Oaks, Western Canada Airways' manager, began to lure young pilots to his company—future pioneers of aviation, such as Fred Stevenson and Punch Dickins. While the jobs were small at first, Oaks eventually landed a huge government contract with the Department of Railways and Canals to ship men and materiel from Cache Lake to Fort Churchill, Ontario. Although the last spike had been driven into Canada's earth some 40 years earlier, Canada's rail system was still expanding on local and national levels. More and more, the government realized the raw mineral and agricultural wealth of the country—grain, timber, oil, gold and nickel. While the airplane was slowly expanding its foothold in the transportation market, the train was still the fastest way to move large amounts of freight from one region of the country to another.

In the contract offered to Western Canada Airways in February 1927, the government wanted Western Canada Airways to ship 12 men and eight tons of supplies to Fort Churchill in order to conduct geological testing to determine whether Churchill was the next best stop for the Hudson Rail line. Oaks ordered two more Fokker Universals specifically for the job and hired Fred Stevenson and Norwegian Bernt Balchen to pilot the planes. Oaks took care of the administrative side, operating out of his "office"—a tent in Hudson, Ontario, with a hand-painted wooden "Western Canada Airways" sign. The lift began in March and had to be completed before spring break-up in April. Flying 30 days straight, the two Fokkers made 27 trips and completed the contract just in the nick of time with little incident. The day after the last trip, the ice along the route began to crack because of the warmer weather.

Oaks also assisted his pilots on a more practical level. In March, he approached Warner and Carmen Elliott, noted sled and boat builders in Sioux Lookout, to design and construct a new kind of ski for his airplanes. Oaks had been constantly frustrated by the lack of quality airplane skis, which frequently cracked at inopportune times. The old-style skis could also freeze to the ice if the temperature plunged low enough, a dilemma solved only by taxiing the plane onto several rows of stout tree branches before parking it for the night. The Elliott brothers accepted Oaks' challenge and manufactured a new ski made of quality hardwood and copper held together by some 1400 rivets.

Oaks also designed the first portable nose hangar for aircrews servicing their planes in cold weather. The hangar consisted of a three-sided canvas tent that shielded the plane's engine and engineer from the elements. It also included a stool and a small stove so that engineers could stay warm and heat the motor oil before putting it into the engine. By 1930, mechanics and engineers across the entire country depended on Doc's portable hangar to complete repairs in less-than-perfect weather conditions.

In 1927, for his efforts in completing the Cache Lake contract and for developing innovative skis and the portable hangar, Oaks was awarded the first McKee Trophy, also called the Trans-Canada Trophy, for meritorious service in the advancement of aviation in Canada. The trophy was named for Dalzell McKee, an American-born pilot who made the first flight of a seaplane across Canada in 1926. An enthusiastic civil pilot, McKee was killed in a 1927 crash in Lac La Peche, Québec. Oaks became the first in a long list of pioneers of Canadian aviation. While accepting the award from the Honorable J.L. Ralston, Minister of Defence, Doc told the assembled guests that the success of his endeavors stemmed not from any sustained effort on his part, but from the committed teamwork and solid work ethic of all the members of the Western Canada Airways crew.

But as much as Oaks accomplished with Western Canada Airways, his heart still belonged to his first love—mining. He was still convinced and told anyone who would listen that the airplane could be brought to bear as an advanced tool in exploiting and cultivating Canada's resources. Oaks again approached James Richardson with his idea for an air service to do aerial surveillance for minerals and supply miners with the necessary equipment to scour Canada's most isolated geography. Richardson agreed and put up close to $600,000 to fund Oaks' newest company, Northern Aerial Minerals Exploration Company (NAME). When the company was officially launched in 1928, Oaks was surprised to receive a letter from Professor Haultain, the professor at the University of Toronto who had given him special permission to do his "flying" thesis. The letter admonished Oaks for not having kept Haultain apprised of his activities and praised him for linking mining and flying and for following through on the ideas in his thesis.

But the organization of the company was complicated. NAME would fly into uncharted territory, to places that had never before been touched by modern man. As a result, a series of fuel caches needed to be established along prospective air routes, caches that could only be delivered by boat and rail, which took time. One shipment that left Hudson in May 1928 was not expected to reach its destination until June 1929!

In August 1928, Oaks and nine other prospectors headed into the Mackenzie River valley in the Northwest Territories in search of the infamous McLeod Mine. The mine, it was rumored, was one of great worth that had been discovered by a single lost prospector who had staked his claim and then forgotten where it was. More than one man had died looking for the mine, and intrigue and rumor abounded that another had been murdered for claiming knowledge of its whereabouts. Oaks, with the assistance of Charles McLeod, a descendant of the mine's founder, flew the area day after day, looking for the mine. Throughout the months of August and September, Oaks circled the Mackenzie River valley, searching for any sign of the lost mine. He was awestruck by the teeming wildlife and lush, green forest of the valley in Canada's North. Unfortunately, none of the wildlife was able to help Oaks find the mine, and on September 15, leery of the changing weather socking him in, Oaks was forced to fly out of the valley. He left the nine prospectors to hike back to civilization, and they arrived in Fort Simpson two weeks later.

In December of that same year, Oaks was scheduled to pick up two prospectors he had left at Richmond Gulf in Ontario the previous summer on the understanding he would return for them in January. He was accompanied on the flight by a pair of newlyweds who were off to the wilds of northern Ontario on their honeymoon, as well as an Anglican missionary and his wife, all on their way to Rupert House, Ontario. The trip started off well enough; they dropped off a load of mail in nearby Moose Factory and continued on. What started off as a clear, cold winter afternoon soon deteriorated into a full-blown blizzard blanketing the plane with snow. Try as he might, Oaks could not see farther than a few feet ahead of the plane, and he soon became disoriented. He descended slowly until the outline of a frozen lake became visible. With conditions continuing to deteriorate and no better option available to them, Oaks swallowed hard and decided to land on the ice to wait out the storm. Bringing all his concentration to bear, with sweat dotting his brow even in such cold, blustery weather, Oaks aimed the plane at the frozen lake. The landing was rough. The plane bounced several times, then evened out, and for a moment, everyone aboard thought they had landed without incident. But a loud crack sounded above the howl of the wind, and Doc knew that one of the plane's skis had cracked.

The five passengers and Oaks huddled in the cabin of the plane to stay warm. The missionary prayed, and the honeymooners cried while holding each other. Outside the wind roared, and darkness fell around them. The temperature plunged below $-40°$ F, and they resorted to putting on all the clothes they had brought with them just to ward off hypothermia. They shivered throughout the night, not sleeping. In the morning, they realized that no one knew where they were, so Oaks left the plane and set out on foot.

The blizzard had died somewhat, but the wind still bit at his face as he slogged through the knee-high snow. He grew tired after an hour but pressed on, licking the ice from his frozen mustache as he walked. After an hour, he looked around and swore that the surrounding area was familiar. Breaking through a tree line, he came face to face with an outcropping of rock that tickled his memory. He smiled in celebration, now knowing exactly where he was. Half an hour later, he trudged into a clearing that contained a wooden cabin with smoke spewing from its chimney and a young dog team running circles around the outside of the cabin and yapping. The door opened, and a fur-wrapped Native man emerged. He stared at Oaks in surprise.

"You look a little cold, Doc!" the Native laughed. Oaks shook his head, too cold and tired to care that the man had used the hated nickname. He warmed himself by the stove, then headed back to the plane while his friend mustered his dog team and set off for help. By sunset that evening, another team arrived, bringing with it a blacksmith from nearby Rupert House. Oaks, as it turned out, had overflown the settlement by more than seven miles during the storm.

The honeymooners, the missionary and his wife gratefully bundled themselves onto the sleds of the assembled dog team and set out for Rupert House. With the help of the blacksmith, Oaks repaired his broken ski and met the prospectors a mere two days into the new year of 1929.

Despite Oaks' enthusiasm and his vision of the airplane as a tool for mining exploration, NAME was not viable as a business. Prospectors could not always pay for their transportation, and the aerial surveying didn't even pay for the gas that went into the planes. Maps were few and often unreliable, so the company was forced to hire Native guides to help

Doc Oaks looks towards the future of aviation in Canada.

navigate. In 1931, Oaks left NAME and started his own company, which he called Oaks Airways.

With two planes, Oaks Airways provided many of the same services Western Canada Airways and NAME had provided, but on a smaller scale. He bought one Fairchild KR-34 for mining reconnaissance and a Junkers JW-34 for freight transport. But again, the financial realities of his vision were complicated.

While the idea was sound and revolutionary for its time, the money to keep Oaks Airways flying was just not there. In 1934, despite having hauled 50 tons of freight across Ontario, Oaks sold the Junkers and focused his business solely on mining reconnaissance, flying prospectors throughout Manitoba and Ontario. But during World War II, Oaks Airways was forced to discontinue its services as Canada focused its energies and money on the war effort.

For the duration of the war, Oaks was hired on by a familiar face, the man who had once tried to save him from a beating at the hands of an irate soldier on the front lines of the Battle of the Somme in 1916. Clark Ruse hired Oaks as a consultant in 1943 for the Clark Ruse Aircraft Company. In 1945, Oaks left Clark Ruse with a warm handshake and a "thank you," and returned to his first love, working as a mining engineer in Port Arthur.

James Richardson came calling again in 1953, hiring Oaks as a consultant for one of his new companies. But soon after agreeing to help out his old friend, Oaks began to think of retirement. He was content with what he had accomplished, although often frustrated by his shortcomings. His vision of linking mining and flying had been difficult to realize, and although he had accomplished much, Doc Oaks was often left to wonder why it hadn't worked out the way he planned. He left flying in 1953, content to spend his golden years basking in the love of his family, but at the same time restless over what could have been.

On July 21, 1968, while living in Toronto, Harold Oaks passed away quietly in his sleep at the age of 71. Canada's aviation officials agreed that this man of vision, such a pioneer of aviation in Canada, was deserving of a high posthumous honor. In 1973, Oaks was inducted into Canada's Aviation Hall of Fame, immortalized in Canadian history by his hated moniker, "Doc." Although he had tried to get away from it his whole life, those who knew him and understood what Oaks had contributed to the country's future never knew him by any other name. In the Aviation Hall of Fame, these words testify to Harold "Doc" Oaks' role in Canadian history:

> The professional daring of his aerial expeditions into uncharted regions led others of his reed to colonize the North and bring outstanding benefits to Canadian aviation.

CHAPTER FOUR

Walter Edwin Gilbert
1899–1986

THE BRIGHT SEPTEMBER SUNSHINE was deceiving. The sun's rays did nothing to warm his chilled bones. The exertion of scrambling over frozen rock, although tiring, also did little to warm him as he scrambled after the rest of his party.

Walter Gilbert gasped in pain as the exposed sole of his foot scraped along another outcropping of rock. He sat down, cradling his scratched and bleeding foot on his leg and pressed it between his hands, trying to warm it.

"Just hang on, then!" he called out to the rest of his crew. "Wouldn't mind taking a bit of a break if we're going to tramp through this godforsaken rock barefoot!"

The three other men in his party stopped and made their way back to Gilbert.

"I'm not much better off, but you don't hear me complaining," grinned Dick Finnie, a filmmaker with the Department of the Interior.

"You've been out here for how many weeks so far?" replied Stan Knight, Gilbert's air engineer. "Your feet are probably used to it!"

"Gents, I'm afraid if we don't keep moving, we're not going to find anything before the sun goes down," fretted Major Lauchie T. Burwash, head of the expedition. "I'm sorry, but we really have to keep moving."

Gilbert groaned aloud, massaging his foot as best he could, then placing it gingerly on the ground as he stood up.

"All right, Burwash. Why don't you move on ahead, and us cripples here will just take our time?"

"Fine by me," Burwash harrumphed, and he marched off.

Gilbert waited a moment, alternating standing on one foot, then the other.

"I wish I'd brought my own damn boots," he mused aloud.

Knight and Finnie shook their heads, and the three set off after the antsy Major Burwash.

The rocks of King William Island's Victory Point were razor sharp, so honed by the fierce weather of Canada's North that they were cutting the explorers' boots to ribbons. The men had been searching for two days and had so far found nothing—no traces, no bodies, no artifacts. Nothing.

Gilbert began choosing his footing more carefully, hopping from one spot to another as he sought out softer bits of ground. Knight chuckled and began to follow his pilot step by step, his boots also looking worse for the wear. They were just beginning to get the hang of it when they heard a sharp whistle. They looked up and saw Burwash 100 yards ahead, waving his hands frantically.

As quickly as their raw feet would allow, the three men rushed over to join Burwash. He stood on an outcropping of rock overlooking the waters off Victory Point. He stood perfectly still, staring at something on the ground. Gilbert stepped up next to Burwash and looked down. It was a piece of cloth, no more than a few inches across. It was navy.

There was only one way a piece of dyed blue cloth could end up this far north. Gilbert's breath caught in his throat as he

Walter Gilbert in his flying cap and parka

~⊙X⊙~

looked up to see the weathered frames of timber and canvas tents, and he began to walk towards the long-abandoned campsite. As he carefully made his way around the site, he noticed more and more items on the ground—a knife here, a bit of iron there, an empty meat tin.

The wind whipped the shreds of the canvas tent, and Gilbert braced himself against a chill that was not just because of the cold. Gilbert and his companions were standing in the company of the dead.

They had found a campsite that belonged to the crew of the expedition of Sir John Franklin, lost almost 90 years earlier.

⚜

Walter Edwin Gilbert was born in Cardinal, Ontario, on March 8, 1899. He was a curious, enthusiastic youngster who thrived under the watchful eye of his parents. So infused with boyish energy and optimism was he that his parents could not deny him when, at the age of 11, he asked—no, demanded— that they take him to Montréal to see his first *aeroplane*!

It was July 27, 1910, and the first Canadian Aviation Meet was being held with much fanfare at the community of Dorval, just outside the city of Montréal, Québec. Walter took the train with his parents and chattered the entire way about what it must be like to fly! Gilbert stood entranced with a crowd of thousands, necks craned upwards, watching the magical flying machines do their work. The highlight of the show was watching Count Jacques de Lesspes set a new record for sustained flight as he looped his rickety Blériot biplane in and around Montréal for exactly 90 minutes.

Although he was enthralled, the impact of the aviation meet on Gilbert was somewhat latent. When asked later if he had been interested in flying since childhood, he confessed in his book *Arctic Pilot*, published in 1940, "Not until I was 18!"

At the age of 18, Gilbert wanted to do what most young men in Canada were doing—go to war. The Allies, buoyed by the entry of the U.S. into World War I, were finally beginning to make some small headway on the trench-scarred plains of France. Gilbert could fathom doing little else, even if his enthusiasm was somewhat tempered by repeatedly hearing news of someone he knew dying overseas. Following his 18th birthday, Gilbert marched into a local recruiting office and proudly informed the desk officer that he was ready to go to war. He was promptly rejected.

Gilbert could not believe that his dreams of adventure and conquest had been shattered simply because his feet were too flat for military standards. He was told that it would be difficult for him to march and run in standard military footwear, but Gilbert would not be consoled.

"I didn't mind. After all, birds have flat feet. But I did want to go to the war!" he later wrote.

Still, Walter could serve his country without packing a rifle. The Imperial Munitions Board in Montréal hired him to be a shrapnel inspector. Although the position paid well and the work was mildly interesting, Gilbert was still inwardly crushed that he could not go to war. His savior, however, came from New York with promises of not only serving overseas, but also being able to fly. A representative of the British Royal Flying Corps was sent to New York to set up a recruiting office. In 1917, he visited Montréal to scout out new bodies to feed the death machine that was the aerial battlefield of Europe. Gilbert signed up and was promptly accepted.

While Walter later turned out to be an excellent pilot, the early stages of his training at Camp Borden left his instructors wondering if he would ever get off the ground. Not that Walter had much help; the Curtiss trainers he was being taught to fly were underpowered, unreliable deathtraps. And even the most unsafe plane was made more lethal by an unsafe pilot. One morning, while practicing landings, Gilbert's instructor so feared for his life that he hopped out of the plane and told Gilbert to take off without him.

"I guess you're going to kill yourself eventually anyway. You might just as well have a go at it right now," the instructor shouted over his shoulder.

But Gilbert defied his instructor's expectations and survived his first solo flight. He was later posted to the Central Flying

School at Upavon, Wiltshire, England, to take the remainder of his courses in gunnery and aerial fighting.

With little warning, he was posted to the battlefield in March 1918. Having overcome the lack of skill that dogged him through the early days of his training, Gilbert stared into the air above the battlefield and stoically resolved to be the best fighter pilot in the skies. He never saw a single battle.

No sooner was he posted overseas than Gilbert fell ill with Spanish influenza, a nasty disease that tore whole companies of soldiers out of the action. Gilbert was deemed unfit for battle. Just when he began to feel better, he contracted pneumonia. And so, by the time he was ready to fly again, the war was over, and he was invalided to England in 1919 not having fired a single shot.

Gilbert stayed on with the newly formed Canadian Air Force (CAF), but it was clear from the outset that the CAF would not endure. With no planes and no available funding, the CAF was disbanded in 1920. Like so many other trained pilots, Gilbert found himself highly skilled but with no way to use his very specific training. No airlines flew in Canada, nor freighting services, and thus there were no employment opportunities for pilots.

Gilbert made his way to Vancouver on a relative's invitation to work in a mine in British Columbia doing surveying and sketching maps. But the hard, dirty work of mining could not compare to the freedom Gilbert felt flying. Eager to share his experiences, in 1923 he formed the International Air Force Club in Vancouver and became its first president. The club was a social group where former pilots could gather and swap stories about their flying days. The club later merged with the Air Force Club of British Columbia. Members enjoyed lectures and presentations from visitors on the state of flight in Canada as well as on new technologies, such as the use of the radio.

But even though the club was a good place to socialize, it just wasn't enough to scratch Gilbert's flying itch. He heard from a friend in Ottawa that the government was reactivating the CAF. On a whim, Gilbert submitted an application and got word shortly afterwards that he was accepted.

Just glad to be back in the air, Gilbert patiently endured a two-month refresher course at Camp Borden before receiving his first assignment. He was posted to northern Manitoba, where he flew forestry patrol, a common use for airplanes in the early days of services like the CAF and the Ontario Provincial Air Service. Gilbert spent hours each day humming along with the roar of his plane's engine, watching out for smoke or flame across northern Manitoba and Saskatchewan.

But by 1928, commercial air services were beginning to spring up across the country. One company in particular, Western Canada Airways, the brainchild of Doc Oaks and James Richardson, now employed such noteworthy pilots as Punch Dickins, Bernt Balchen and Fred Stevenson. He might have been intimidated by some of the names associated with WCA, but Gilbert made some cautious inquiries about employment with the company. In November 1928, he was hired as one of WCA's pilots.

He spent two years flying for the WCA, mostly flying mining prospectors and freight throughout northern British Columbia. The plane, as it turned out, was the chariot that blazed a path into some of Canada's most remote wastelands, where oil, coal, gold and silver lay beneath the rocky, snow-choked land waiting to be discovered.

In the summer of 1929, Gilbert successfully transported two grizzled prospectors into a stand of mountains in southern Alaska that would have been virtually inaccessible by land. He chuckled to himself in the pilot's seat, as Tim Williams, one of the prospectors, counted off the days it would have taken to get to their claim if they'd gone overland.

Walter Gilbert in 1928

～◐Ｃ◑～

"There's another day," he said in disbelief, and two hours later, "and another day—"

In December 1929, Gilbert got word that he and Jeanne, his wife of almost two years, were being transferred to Fort McMurray in northern Alberta. The North was an unending bank of mineral deposits, its most desolate reaches brimming with oil, gold, silver and other precious minerals. Planes and pilots were in high demand as companies and prospectors raced north in the hopes of striking it rich.

Walter and Jeanne arrived in Fort McMurray on January 1, 1930. After a two-week stay at the Franklin Hotel, the pair bought a two-bedroom house just behind the hotel. But neither was prepared for the ferocity of the cold so far north. On one occasion, housebound for several days because of the weather and needing an outlet for her energy, Jeanne decided to varnish the floors and walls of their house. The next day, while admiring her work, Jeanne noticed the varnish trickling down the walls and pooling around her slippers. It hadn't dried; it had frozen!

Later that June, Gilbert made his first trip to Aklavik, a small Hudson's Bay Company (HBC) settlement on the coast of the Arctic Ocean in the Yukon. Following the Mackenzie River route, Gilbert flew as far as he could, paying little attention to the time. Feeling sleepy, he looked at his watch and wondered why he was so tired if it was only 2:30 in the afternoon. Then it struck him—it was 2:30 in the morning! Never having experienced "the land of the midnight sun," he had not noticed that the sun hadn't set. He had been flying for almost 18 hours!

Gilbert was disappointed in Aklavik. He had come to love the North, especially the sight of it from the sky. He was never more happy or more at peace than when slicing his way through the peaks of snowcapped mountains or squinting against the glare of the sun against the impossibly blue sky. The world around him was frozen in magnificent beauty, and he reveled in it.

But Aklavik was different. Dirty, rickety and small, the community was made up of a few small, ramshackle cabins. In June, with snow and ice still ringing the coast, it seemed even more soulless than ever. The thought of living there in the depths of winter, with –60° F temperatures and constant darkness, made his heart ache with loneliness.

Jeanne Gilbert often flew with husband Walter.

But there were plenty of people around, including two young entrepreneurs who sought out Gilbert just hours after his landing. They were salesmen, trying hard to hawk their wares to the communities of the North. They tried to foist everything, from the latest conveniences to food and supplies, on the local residents of Aklavik. Unfortunately, they found few buyers. Determined to carve out a niche for their products,

the pair decided to set off for Herschel Island, the most northern trading post at the time, located on a tiny pinprick of land
in the Arctic Ocean. With time on his hands, Gilbert agreed to
help them, and the next day, flew the two salesmen north to
the former whaling station.

Bold in action and enthusiastic in their endeavors, the
salesmen came up empty-handed. Although the local Inuit
were impressed with the goods, they could not imagine having to wait a year for the next supply ship to deliver their pur-
chases. Despite the enthusiastic, even desperate appeals of the
two salesmen, the Inuit left, chuckling as they tramped off into
the snow.

Having marked the first commercial flight to Herschel
Island, Gilbert returned home to a new adventure. When he
was called into the office of the Supervisor of the Mackenzie
River District and given his instructions for an upcoming
charter, Gilbert could scarcely believe what was being asked
of him. He felt goose bumps dot his skin as he listened in
rapt fascination to a story that he—and *everyone*—knew so
very well.

By 1845, few lands of the world hadn't been explored.
Throughout the 17th and 18th centuries, the British, French
and Portuguese had rushed out to all corners of the globe by
ship in search of raw materials such as spices, gold, furs, timber
and fish. These intrepid explorers found passages to such lands
on the continents of North and South America, Asia and Australia and founded colonies on these new lands. It was in the
name of commerce that the world had been explored, but
there was one mystery that still evaded the hardiest of explorers—the Northwest Passage. Jacques Cartier had searched for it,
as had Columbus—a path across the top of the world, straight
to the spice and silk of the Orient. If such a passage could be
found, it would be an economic boon for the nation that could
navigate it.

On May 26, 1845, 60-year-old Sir John Franklin left England in the company of 128 men and officers. Piloting the ships *Terror* and *Erebus*, Franklin and his men set their sights on the North in the hope of uncovering the as-yet-undiscovered Northwest Passage. They were last seen by a whaling ship on July 26, 1845, moored to an iceberg just outside Baffin Bay, waiting for the ice to thin enough that they could make their way west. They were never heard from again.

By 1854, nearly a dozen searches had been launched for the party with few results. At the campsite of the crew's first wintering, three gravesites and several empty meat tins were all that could be found of the ill-fated expedition. But there was talk among the Inuit. One Native in particular recalled seeing a group of 40 white men struggling through the snow, pulling sledges and boats full of supplies. Still, no traces of Franklin's remains could be found, nor the bulk of his crew.

Lord Leopold M'Clintock, who led several expeditions in search of the party throughout the 1850s, uncovered the most useful information. In 1858, camped out along the coast of King William Island, M'Clintock discovered a scrap of paper with a note written by one of Franklin's officers, Captain F.M. Crozier. According to Crozier, the ships had become locked in the ice on September 12, 1846, and were never freed, and Franklin died June 11, 1847. The note, dated April 25, 1848, stated that the remaining crew abandoned ship and set out for a Hudson's Bay Company outpost at Back's Fish River, a 250-mile journey on foot. None made it alive.

Stories circulated of the Inuit finding one of the ships and seeing bunks full of frozen corpses. Several Natives even produced medals and hats that had, at some point, belonged to sailors from the expedition. It was rumored that Franklin's corpse had been set against a rocky bluff on King William Island, looking out over the North that had, in the end, defeated him. Still, despite many attempts, no one ever found him.

But in 1930, the Canadian government thought that it had. Having purchased a document from an old sailor that seemed to indicate the whereabouts of Franklin's grave on King William Island, the government hired one of its own explorers, Major Lauchie T. Burwash, to track it down. Gilbert and his engineer Stan Knight were hired to fly him there. The trio was also to photograph as much of the northern coastline as possible for the purposes of mapping. Their plane was outfitted with an aerial camera and a new invention, a portable radio, which could be used to communicate with the home base.

The party arrived in Coppermine, a settlement on the northern coast of the Northwest Territories, in early August 1930. Also accompanying the party was another WCA pilot, Buck Buchanan, charged with recovering "SK," one of the most storied planes in the history of Canadian commercial aviation.

On August 24, 1929, Colonel C.D.H. MacAlpine of Dominion Explorers started out on a prospecting trip that was to cover thousands of miles of the North, from Winnipeg to Baker Lake, Aklavik, Fort Norman and Great Bear Lake. The party of eight men and two planes ended up stranded in the NWT for more than two months before hiking 70 miles over the frozen surface of the Arctic Ocean to the nearest outpost. SK had been one of the planes used on the mission. She had been left behind on the shore of Queen Maud Gulf, her cabin key entrusted to a camp of Inuit who lived nearby. She sat there for an entire year, exposed to Canada's harshest climate.

With time to spare before the annual supply ship arrived at Coppermine with a large shipment of supplies for the trip to King William Island, Gilbert and Buchanan set out to look for SK. Leaving Burwash at Coppermine, the two pilots followed the flight path taken by the MacAlpine expedition a year earlier and were startled to find faithful, intrepid SK, still moored exactly where the party had abandoned her.

"There's one plane that's spent a cold, lonely winter," Gilbert muttered, as he brought his plane in for a landing.

As surprised as Buchanan and Gilbert were to find the plane in place and relatively intact, neither was prepared for what happened next. Checking over the plane and deeming it flightworthy despite a set of rusty control cables, the two men shrugged at one another and decided to try to start up SK. Adding some oil to the engine and some fuel to the gas tanks, both men started in surprise when the engine caught on the first try.

"Someone's eager to get back home!" Buchanan yelled over the roar of the old workhorse of the Arctic.

With nighttime coming on, the two men set up camp for the night. As Gilbert munched on fruit from a can, Buchanan decided to brave the cool northern temperatures for a bath in the freezing waters of the gulf. Just as he stripped down to his skin and began the dash to the water, a crowd of people appeared, seemingly out of nowhere. A group of local Inuit stood transfixed, staring at Buchanan's nudity.

"All right then! That's enough!" Buchanan said hotly, wrapping his arms around himself in a poor attempt to cover his nakedness. The Inuit women snickered as Buck edged his way back to the plane and scrambled into his clothes. Shaking with laughter, Gilbert greeted their visitors. He invited them to sit and talk, but became confused when one Inuit held out his closed fist and opened it. Nestled in the man's pink palm was the key to the cabin of SK.

Gilbert and Buck had managed to pry their way in without the key, and Gilbert was amazed the Inuit had hung onto it for so long. Despite Gilbert's offerings of food and conversation the Inuit melted into the night, leaving Buck feeling somewhat peevish and Gilbert completely amazed.

Once they returned to Coppermine, Buck fueled SK and took off for Fort McMurray. Knight, Gilbert and Burwash spent the remainder of that day making preparations and cramming as many supplies they could into the plane. The next morning, a beautiful, clear morning, the trio hopped into the plane, intending to begin their mission and ready for whatever challenges awaited them.

On takeoff, a great plume of smoke rose from the engine. Gilbert was forced to abort takeoff and, with Stan Knight at his side and Burwash fretting at a respectable distance, Gilbert quickly located the problem. One of the engine's pistons was blown. It was a repair they could only make with the proper tools, parts and facilities.

But all was not lost. They needed only to get word to Canadian Airways, successor to WCA in 1930, to send a replacement aircraft. Unfortunately, the radio set aboard the aircraft would not work. Gilbert remembered that the supply ship *Bay Chimo* had a radio set aboard, and he ran after her just as the ship was edging away from the coastline. He made a quick radio call to headquarters in Winnipeg to send a replacement craft for the Burwash expedition.

The next day, the roar of a plane roused Gilbert from a nap in one of the company's guestrooms. Gilbert grabbed a pair of "water boots" an Inuit had traded him and rushed out the door to see who had arrived. As the plane taxied to a stop, Gilbert laughed as he recognized the pilot and the plane. It was none other than Buchanan and the stalwart SK.

With new control wires and a full tank of gas, SK flew like a dream, and Burwash, Knight and Gilbert were quick to take off on their mission. But soon after they left Coppermine, a howling blizzard forced them down at the tiny trading community of Bernard Harbor for an entire week. Once the storm subsided, the trio headed back into the air, winging their way along the northern coastline, photographing every square foot with the aerial camera. Just after noon that day, they put down for more supplies and fuel at Cambridge Bay, east of

Coppermine. They spent the night there and were entertained at a community dinner held by the staff of the HBC trading post. They were celebrating the arrival of the annual supply ship. One particular delicacy featured at dinner was rarely seen up north—eggs. Several crates of eggs packed in rock salt had arrived on the ship, and the staff of the HBC outpost had hard-boiled them and served them at dinner.

Gilbert deftly cracked and peeled an egg, but recoiled as his nose caught the first whiff of it.

"These bloody eggs are rotten," he whispered to Knight.

"At least you smelled yours first," Knight mumbled through a mouthful of egg, a disgusted look on his face.

Gilbert looked up, ready to raise the point with the others, but stopped. The rest of the HBC staff had four, even five eggs on their plates and were mowing them down with great gusto. Gilbert shrugged and popped the egg into his mouth.

The next morning, the crew set off for their ultimate destination—King William Island. No sooner had they left the relatively sheltered cove of Cambridge Bay than great chunks of ice began to appear in the water below. Flying over the island, Gilbert could not believe the rocky, barren chunk of rock could ever have been home to more than 100 sailors for three years.

Electing to put down for the night, the crew landed at Peterson Bay, on the southern tip of the island. There they refueled from a cache that had been established before the flight and picked up the fourth member of their party: Dick Finnie, from Canada's Department of the Interior, who was currently making a movie about life in the North. A gregarious, outgoing sort, Finnie was a welcome addition to the quiet dignity of Major Burwash.

The crew took off early the next morning, making its way around the coast of King William Island towards Victory Point. Just as they rounded the southern tip and came north, Gilbert stared down at his compass, which was swinging wildly in circles. He looked over his shoulder and nodded at Knight, who began snapping photos. He looked up a few minutes later and gave Gilbert a thumbs-up. The crew had just photographed the Northern Magnetic Pole, and were the first to ever do so.

Reaching Victoria Point by early afternoon, Gilbert and the crew put down on an ice-free inlet close to the coast and made their way ashore. Burwash was eager to get moving, so he and Finnie set off to explore the surrounding area while Knight and Gilbert set up the campsite. Finnie and Burwash returned hours later, declaring no success. The next morning, the entire team set off in search of Franklin's remains.

It was not easy going. The sharp, rocky outcroppings they were forced to scramble over took a heavy toll on their footwear, slicing the whale-skin boots to ribbons. Before long, Gilbert was hopping from one soft spot to the next in an effort to protect his cracked and bleeding feet. When he looked up, Burwash was waving frantically to the rest of the party from about 100 yards ahead. He had found something.

The team quietly and reverently picked their way through the 85-year-old campsite. It was a somber moment, the living realizing that they were disturbing the soil of the dead. They found bits of iron, a fragment of navy blue cloth, empty meat tins and other artifacts that confirmed this as a previously undiscovered campsite of the Franklin expedition.

But try as they might, they could not find Franklin's remains. At the edge of the campsite, Gilbert said a quiet prayer for the abandoned souls of the ill-fated voyage. Burwash collected as many artifacts as he could, and the four made their way back to their campsite.

Once in the air, Gilbert completed a circle of the island, and Knight photographed the entire coastline. Back in Coppermine the next day, they told their story to the men gathered at the small northern settlement, who listened in rapt fascination.

The next day, the crew set a course for home, stopping in Fort Smith to use the settlement's radio and send word to home base of their return. The response surprised Gilbert. The press, it seemed, had taken the party's three-week silence to mean that they had been lost to the North, succumbing to the elements or to a horrible, fiery crash. After requesting that word be sent to his wife that he was not dead, Gilbert and his party headed back to Fort McMurray, where they were welcomed as heroes. In 1933, Gilbert would be awarded the McKee Trophy for this flight, "in recognition of his exploratory flights throughout the North." The award was the second in as many years; in 1932, Gilbert was also made a fellow of the Royal Geographic Society, a high honor indeed.

Upon his return home, Gilbert settled into a life of relative normalcy, for a bush pilot. He flew freight out of Fort McMurray for mining companies and prospectors throughout the North. In March 1931, he and Punch Dickins made the first ever commercial flight to Port Radium on Great Bear Lake, the site of a huge silver, radium, manganese and cobalt strike.

Gilbert's cargo was not always freight. On one occasion, one of the miners at Great Bear Lake hired him to fly the man's wife to the mine for a visit. When Gilbert and the woman arrived, they learned the miner's cabin had burned to the ground earlier that day. The woman spent a mere two and a half hours with her husband before returning home with Gilbert at the end of the day.

There was still some excitement in Gilbert's life. In August 1931, Gilbert was contracted by Canada Press to fly a reporter to Aklavik for a rendezvous with Charles and Anne Morrow Lindbergh. In 1927, Charles was elevated to the status of North America's first hero of the 20th century when he became the first man to fly nonstop from New York to Paris. In just 33 1/2 hours, Lindbergh piloted his tiny monoplane, the *Spirit of St. Louis*, over the sprawling blue of the Atlantic Ocean and onto a tiny airfield just outside Paris. This time, in the company of his beautiful wife, Lindbergh was bound for the Orient, flying across northern Canada to get there.

The Lindberghs did indeed stop in Aklavik, and the reporter Gilbert had flown there got his chance to sit down with the famous flyer. The next day, when Lindbergh had trouble getting his fully fueled plane off the waters of the Arctic Ocean, Gilbert started up his own plane and pulled ahead of the Lindberghs' plane. Opening the throttle to full, the speed of Gilbert's plane generated enough of a slipstream to help Charles pull his wallowing aircraft into the sky.

Throughout 1932, Gilbert continued his flights into the North, flying men and materiel to camps in the cold, Barren Lands. In June of that year, he and engineer Lew Parmenter were charged with the task of flying the Bishop of the Arctic to Aklavik and then to nearby Shingle Point for a tour of the missions in the North. After stopping in Aklavik to pick up two bags of mail, the trio continued on to their ultimate destination. Despite it being summer, ice still jammed the waters in and around Shingle Point, and with the Fokker on pontoons, Gilbert was unable to land. Instead, he ordered Lew to drop the bags of mail onto the island through a specially designed chute at the rear of the plane.

As Gilbert circled the tiny settlement, Parmenter dutifully tossed both bags of mail down the chute and watched as each landed in a puff of snow on the ground below. Gilbert then looked over his shoulder and saw a third mailbag sitting in the rear of the plane.

"Hey, Lew!" he yelled over the drone of the plane's engine. "That one too, eh?"

"But Walter, I don't think—"

"No kidding! Just do it!" Gilbert cut him off.

Parmenter shrugged and dropped the third bag out of the chute, then climbed back into his seat beside Walter.

Charles Lindbergh (center) shares a moment with Walter Gilbert (right) and Lew Parmenter in August 1931. Five months earlier, Lindbergh's nine-month-old son, Charles Lindbergh, Jr., was abducted from the Lindbergh home in Hopewell, New Jersey. A ransom note was found in the baby's crib. Even though the Lindbergs repeatedly tried to pay the ransom, the infant's partially decomposed body was found two months later a half-mile from the Lindbergh's home. Richard Hauptmann was later arrested and executed for the kidnapping and murder, although questions remain to this day as to whether he was responsible for the infant's death.

"I think there's going to be hell to pay this time, Walter,"
Parmenter laughed. "That bag had the padre's clothes and
shaving kit in it."

Gilbert continued flying throughout the 1930s, carrying
furs, dynamite, equipment and machinery throughout
Canada's North. By the time World War II had begun in
Europe, Walter had moved up in the world. Canadian Pacific
Airlines bought Canadian Airlines in 1942, and Gilbert was
named Superintendent of Vancouver, then of the Mackenzie
River District.

But Gilbert's heart still belonged in British Columbia, and
in 1945, he and his good friend Russ Baker started their own
airline, Central British Columbia Airways, flying out of Fort St.
John. He flew much the same cargo as he had during his time
with WCA, but Gilbert was unable to attract enough business
to make the airline profitable. And anyway, his heart just wasn't
in it. He had excelled in the skies, establishing an impeccable
safety record without a single crash on his record. He had seen
sights other men could only dream of, had hunted for the
bones of Sir John Franklin and had been to the Magnetic North
Pole. At 46, Gilbert was content with all he had done in his
life and, in 1949, sold off his shares in Central BC Airways.

But Gilbert always remained connected to flying. In 1949,
he started up a fishing resort in the BC interior near Chilliwack
Lakes. He designed the resort to be isolated so that patrons
would have to fly in to fish. The resort became a popular get-
away for other bush pilots in BC, and hardly a weekend went
by when Gilbert wasn't sitting around a campfire, swapping
stories with another pilot who had dropped in to enjoy his
hospitality. But the resort wasn't profitable, and business
wasn't as steady as he'd hoped. Gilbert was further motivated
to sell the property after a young lawyer from California offered
him a hefty sum.

Gilbert moved to Washington, where he started up his own real estate brokerage, Walter Gilbert Realty. He lived out the rest of his life in a quiet existence with Jeanne by his side. In 1973, he was one of the first pilots inducted into Canada's Aviation Hall of Fame. The long list of awards and honors were fitting tribute to a man who gave so much to the development of aviation in Canada and to the development of the North.

On June 18, 1986, Walter Edwin Gilbert passed away in Washington State.

CHAPTER FIVE

Fredrick "Steve" J. Stevenson
1896–1928

He was always smiling when it started, smiling with joy as he put his Avro biplane through its paces, looping above the skies of Fort Frances, Ontario. Sometimes he saw himself laughing, and he saw Frank Ellis, his engineer and good friend, laughing in the seat beside him.

Up and up they climbed in the sky, so high he swore he saw stars, then Fredrick Stevenson snapped the plane around in a barrel roll. Frank reached out and grabbed onto the dash to steady himself, and Steve laughed again.

"Careful, Steve! I had a big lunch!" Frank said.

He pulled back on the stick hard and pulled the plane straight up in the air, then over onto its back. Instead of leveling off, he continued the dive towards the ground. He kept the power low, so his speed was manageable, and spiraled the plane around and around. A few hundred feet later, he pushed the throttle in for full power to pull out of the dive.

But the plane didn't respond. It never did. The engine just grumbled at low power and continued to fall, faster and faster. Frank shouted at him but he couldn't hear over the rushing of wind. His

*breathing quickened, his pulse raced and his spine tingled in terror as
the ground came closer and closer.*

"Frank? What do I do, Frank?" Steve yelled.

*But he still couldn't hear what Frank was saying. Desperately,
he worked the throttle but the engine wouldn't respond. They were so
close to the ground, he could make out the spectators. He thought to
level off and glide back down to the ground, but suddenly the plane
pitched forward even farther. He saw Frank jam his head between
his knees and Steve always found himself wondering if that was
really going to help.*

Steve screamed as the ground rushed up to meet him.

He sat bolt upright in bed, screaming at the top of his lungs.
When he opened his eyes, he saw nothing. He felt wet all over,
and his heart hammered inside him.

He panted in the darkness, looking around. Ahead of him,
through a window, he saw the twinkling stars in the night sky.
All around him was steel, and the air was cold. He was in his
plane, he remembered. He ran a hand through his sweat-
soaked hair and began to breathe deeply. It was just the nightmare again. He was alive.

He heard something outside the plane and held his breath.
It sounded wet and heavy. Snow crunched, and something
snorted. A plaintive, mournful howl sang out right beside his
head, on the other side of the steel skin. It was joined by several
more, each farther away than the one before it. They echoed off
the night sky, surrounding him.

He felt around in the dark, and his fingers recognized his
rifle. He worked the action in the dark and heard a round snake
into the chamber. He sat upright, barely breathing, waiting.
One by one, the wolves ceased howling—another snort, then
the crunch of footsteps fading into the distance.

He lay back down, cradling his rifle. He waited, listening as
intently as he could, but heard only a wisp of wind. Slowly, he

began to relax. He stared up at the roof of the plane, waiting for the wolves to return. The next thing he knew, the sun was rising.

◦◦◆◦◦

The first day Fred Stevenson spent in Europe, he knew he wanted to fly. He hadn't seen an actual airplane until he got to France as a soldier with the 196th University Battalion from Winnipeg, Manitoba. Born in 1896 in Perry Sound, Ontario, to Irish parents, Fred's family had moved to Winnipeg when he was young. As he grew, he heard more and more about airplanes, machines that flew like birds in the sky, but he'd never seen one for himself. In school, a photograph of a biplane circulated in one of his classes, the airplane framed against rolling fields and gray-sky backdrop. But as hard as he tried, he just couldn't quite get enough from the photo. It was great, but it didn't quite capture the experience enough for the quiet, introspective youngster. He needed to see it for himself, evaluate the new machine with his own eyes. He believed that people could fly. He just wasn't sure this was the best way.

In 1914, when Steve was 18, he was taking classes at Wesley College in Winnipeg when the Archduke of Austria was assassinated, and World War I began. At first, almost imperceptibly, but then more noticeably, the male population at the college began to dwindle. There was talk of great adventure, courage in battle and killing Germans. But as the body count from the Great War climbed, talk grew more somber. Each time he spoke with his mother, she told Fred about a childhood acquaintance who was never coming home. He attended several funeral services and, in an odd, perverse kind of logic, the appeal of war began to grow for the young man. College life was growing stale, and his classes, while stimulating, were too general, and he lacked focus. Fred did not know what he was going to do with his life, so why not take part in the great adventure, even if that great adventure was slowly becoming a body factory.

He enlisted with 196th University Battalion at Winnipeg and, after basic training, was shipped to France with the infantry. The front was as depressing as he had heard, but Steve's imagination was captured when he first saw members of the Royal Flying Corps take to the sky. He watched the sky above the battlefield as these 20th-century knights of the air dueled mercilessly in the sky above, twisting, turning, firing, even colliding. Aircraft dropped from the sky like raindrops, crashing into the ground below. Almost no one survived those crashes, but Steve was undaunted. The open sky beckoned him, and he began to pester his commanding officers to allow him to join the ranks of the Canadian Flying Corps. It was a gray, rainy day when an officer in his battalion informed him that he was being transferred to the Royal Flying Corps.

"It's your health," the officer told him in parting.

Because of the novelty of aircraft, the fighter pilot was fast becoming the new knight of a war that was no longer honorable. This reverence, however, belied the fact that the world of aerial combat was a body mill. Both the Allies and Germans worked hard to keep enough planes in the air—and enough men in the planes—to be able to counter the other's air forces. The planes were unreliable and often faulty. They were made of wood and easily penetrated by bullets. There were no parachutes or flak jackets. If a pilot went down, all he could do was pray. And it seemed that God was hearing few prayers.

Stevenson was shipped to England in 1917 to begin fighter training. For two fantastic months, his dream exploded into reality. He learned how to take off, land, steer and shoot. He practiced rolling, banking and diving in slow, decrepit trainer aircraft that forced him to execute all his maneuvers exactly lest he plant himself in the ground. Even at flight school, funerals occurred. Not everyone had the skill to fly, and few walked away from their mistakes.

As soon as his training was completed, he was shipped to France to fight in the skies above Europe. The tide of war was changing. The Russian Empire had fallen to the Communist revolution of October 1917, and the Americans now supported the tired Europeans along the Western Front. Stevenson was assigned the newest, fastest fighter in the entire Royal Flying Corps, the Dolphin. With its twin machine guns and blazing speed, Steve took to the skies, raining bullets down on scores of enemy aircraft. He was not ruthless, just efficient. He accepted the rigors of battle and showed no mercy to those he fought. He was not showy; he was not acrobatic; he simply did his job and did it well.

By war's end, he had been promoted to captain and was awarded the Distinguished Flying Cross and the Croix de Guerre for his skill and bravery. He was credited with the destruction of 18 enemy aircraft and three observation balloons, but most importantly, he returned home from the war without a scratch. His plane took more than a few hits, but it always got him back home to fight another day.

Because of his accomplishments, he was selected at war's end to ferry diplomats between London and France for peace talks. It was tedious work, simple flights with stodgy, often frightened public servants who were quiet and unfriendly. But Steve did his job with the same unflinching professionalism he displayed on the aerial battlefield.

In Russia, all was chaos. Civil war claimed thousands of lives as the Whites, those who favored a return to the monarchy, battled the Communists (the Reds) across the entire country. The Communists under Lenin seized power in 1917 and were forcing communism on the people. It was a concept few living outside St. Petersburg had ever heard of, let alone understood. The Allies watched as the monarchy fell and the Communists withdrew Russia from the war. Quietly, western democracies rallied support for the Whites, providing equipment and instruction for the White forces.

Fred Stevenson signed up to instruct Russian pilots and instantly regretted it. Few of the pilots he trained proved capable of taking off and landing without assistance, and Steve's perfect flight record was nearly ruined dozens of times by inept students. And the Russian climate was terribly cold, so much so that his machines often could not fly. He demanded a great deal of his students, and few could handle it. One week after grudgingly allowing the first of a series of solo flights during which no one (thankfully) died, Steve received word that he was being pulled out of Russia. The Reds were winning, and the situation was too volatile. Steve flew out of Russia, relief growing the farther away he flew.

Returning to Canada in 1920, he found work quite quickly as a pilot with the Canadian Aircraft Company. He was paired with engineer Frank Ellis, and the two barnstormed across western Canada, treating hundreds to aerial acrobatics at exhibitions across the country. For $10 per ride, Frank and Steve took frightened men, women and children up into the air. Some would scream, some would laugh and some would sit silently, white with fear, while Frank and Steve laughed at their expense. Steve often waited for his passengers to relax, then looped the plane upside-down to watch their passengers' reactions.

"If he gets sick, you're the one who gets to clean it up," Frank would say.

Wherever they flew, the two attracted huge crowds. In celebration of their flight, towns held dances to which the two were often invited. One night in central Manitoba, both Frank and Steve were guests at a dance at the local town hall. When they landed at the end of the day, Frank hopped out of the plane and turned to Steve.

"So Steve, we got this dance tonight. You know, girls, music."

Steve wiped his forehead as Frank talked, smearing grease along his brow.

"What's your point, Frank?"

"Did you bring a change of clothes?" Frank asked outright. Steve stopped, looked at his hands, then stared down at his oil-stained coveralls. He started to laugh because he had not thought to bring clean clothes.

"Looks aren't everything, Frank."

And so the two appeared at the door of the dance and, at first, received nothing but stares because of their disheveled appearance. Before long, Steve's charm and dancing skills caught the eyes of many of the women in attendance. Frank sat at the back of the hall, chuckling as pretty women roamed the dance floor, now sporting greasy handprints all over their best dresses.

August 25, 1920, was a beautiful day in Fort Frances, Ontario, as Frank and Steve took to the skies to delight the locals. Up and down, over and around they flew, laughing with joy. After one barrel roll, Steve pulled the plane into a loop-de-loop and dove for the ground, spiraling the plane around and around as he descended. He pumped the throttles in and out, blasting the cylinders with fuel to ensure the engine would respond when he needed it. At 1500 feet, he pushed the throttles in. Nothing happened.

"Frank?" Steve shouted in alarm. They continued spiraling downwards, the engine rumbling at low power despite the throttles being jammed to the stops. Telegraph wires and rail lines became visible as they continued their descent.

"Did you blast the throttles on the way down?" Frank yelled above the rising rush of wind.

"Of course, I did!" Steve hollered back. He pulled back on the stick with all his strength, trying to force the plane out of its dive. He willed the engine to take fuel and roar with power, giving him the speed to resume level flight, but still nothing.

"What do I do, Frank?" Steve yelled.

"Blast it again! C'mon Steve, kick that pig!"

Steve worked the throttle desperately as the altimeter wound down to 200 feet. He pumped and pumped, watching as the ground filled the windscreen. The engine rumbled, then choked, and the plane pitched forward once more. Frank bent forward in his seat, jamming his head between his knees.

When Steve awoke, he felt pain. He tried to open his mouth but couldn't. Finally, he opened his eyes, seeing a white ceiling.

"Steve?" A voice called as an image swam into view.

Steve turned his head and moaned in pain. He saw Frank hovering over him, grinning widely.

He tried to speak again, but his mouth still wouldn't move.

"Steve, you got the worst of that one, let me tell you. I mean, you ended your perfect flying record with a bang," Frank said.

Steve blinked.

"If you're wondering why you can't talk, it's because your jaw is wired shut. Broken. Oh, so is your ankle, and you dislocated your hip. Banged your head up pretty good, too. You're looking darn ugly."

Steve tried to chuckle but coughed instead. He grimaced as pain shot through his face.

"Believe it or not, I walked away from that one," said Frank, twirling in a circle, arms outstretched. "I guess you broke my fall. Took us a few minutes to pry you out of there. Doc says you won't be flying for a while, but that you should recover just fine."

In his mind's eye, Steve watched the crash over and over again. He heard himself scream as the ground rushed up towards him.

Frank clapped his shoulder and leaned in.

"Try to forget about it, okay?"

Fred Stevenson didn't fly for almost three years. His rehabilitation was long and painful. He lost weight because he couldn't eat, and his left leg shrank because he couldn't walk. When his bones healed, he was left with a permanent limp. While his body slowly began to heal itself, his mind did not. He dreamed of the accident repeatedly, waking at the point of impact soaked in sweat and panting heavily. The nightmares belied the truth that he had never needed luck before. Consequently, he began to think that luck had nothing to do with good flying. His crash had robbed him of that naïveté. He plied his loss with liquor and railed against his inability to overcome his fear. Now that he had crashed, his confidence was shaken, and he did not fly again until the Ontario provincial government came knocking at his door.

In 1924, Steve stepped into an airplane again for the first time since his accident as a member of the Ontario Provincial Air Service. For the next two years his eyes scoured the forests of the Canadian Shield on air patrol, spotting fires and delivering supplies to remote outposts in an old HS-2L Flying Boat purchased from the United States. It was a simple existence, spending his days aloft with nowhere to go but straight ahead. The routine helped him recover. His confidence returned, but his once-relaxed demeanor was now gruff and focused. He spent his nights on the loose in whatever town he was stationed, cutting wide swaths through the hearts of the local women. He was lively and spirited and well liked, but he was often irresponsible.

One day, his supervisor at OPAS, Roy Maxwell, called Steve into his office to "have a chat about something." When he sat down in front of Roy's desk, Roy simply handed Steve a sheet of paper. It was a letter from Jim Lyons, the provincial minister responsible for the OPAS, in which the minister expressed his growing irritation with Steve for not having settled his debts with his former landlady in Toronto.

Fred Stevenson in 1926

~⦿~

"If some of the statements made in writing by Mrs. Johnson are at all true, especially with reference to the condition he left the house in, the number of empty liquor bottles and the display of discarded ladies' hose, it is my opinion that the less said about the matter publicly, the better," the letter stated.

Were it not for his beard, Steve would have blushed visibly.

"I trust you'll take care of this, Steve?" Roy asked, pointedly.

Steve nodded, and Roy never heard from the minister again. Two years after he began flying with the OPAS, another opportunity sought him out. Doc Oaks, considered a pioneer of aviation even in his own time, came looking for Steve to join him at Western Canada Airways (WCA). It seemed to be the right time to sign on with a carrier. The North was beginning to swell with surveyors as oil replaced gold as the focus of men's dreams. The government was reaching out to the citizens of its farthest reaches, and the airplane was proving an effective tool in transportation, exploration and mapping. More freight could be moved faster by plane than by dogsled. Pilots were slicing Canada into manageable chunks, and Steve jumped at the opportunity.

His timing could not have been better. Canada was enjoying the perks of a post-war economic boom. Automobiles were cheaper, and their technology was being harvested by other manufacturers to develop machines for farmers, miners and heavy industry. Southern Ontario emerged as a manufacturing and industrial heartland, while the Prairies churned out bumper crops of grain year after year. Wheat quickly became Canada's chief export to Europe, and to ship it overseas as quickly as possible, the government explored the idea of establishing a rail line from Winnipeg to Fort Churchill on Hudson Bay. Ships could then take on cargo at Fort Churchill and have quicker access to Europe via the Arctic Ocean, rather than transporting the wheat to the Maritimes for shipping.

Surrounded by miles of frozen wasteland, the port of Fort Churchill was isolated from any ground transportation. In order to begin geological testing to determine if the rail line could be completed as planned, eight tons of equipment and 14 men had to be transported to Fort Churchill. In March, the Department of Railways and Canals offered Western Canada Airways a contract to haul the men and equipment by air. All the materiel and men needed to be in place before spring break-up on the Hudson Bay in April.

Western Canada Airways purchased two new Fokker Super Universals and began hauling freight. Steve and Bernt Balchen, a Norwegian, were the pilots, and Al Cheesman served as their mechanic. They set up camp of shacks and tents at Cache Lake, Ontario, and flew every day, hauling machinery, provisions and men into northern Manitoba.

Not everyone who came to work for WCA was cut out for such rustic living. The day Bernt Balchen arrived, he was shown to a shack where all the men in camp were huddled around the stove, trying to keep warm. Stevenson was reclining in a chair, smoking his pipe and thumbing through an Eaton's catalog. Suddenly, a young man, barely a boy, covered in grease smudges looked up from where he was warming his hands and asked where the bathroom was.

Stevenson stood up, walked to the door and threw it open. He tore a page out of the catalog he was reading and held it out to the boy.

"The whole world's your bathroom, sonny boy," he boomed. "And if you can't help yourself, then you're no man for this country."

On another occasion, Steve returned to camp from Churchill alone. Balchen had taken on a bad tank of gas at Churchill and was forced to stay behind to repair the problem. It was late afternoon, cold and gray as Stevenson flew home. He shivered in the chill spring air and felt his beard freezing more and more with every breath.

Suddenly, the engine of his plane began to smoke and sputter. Steve checked his instruments to no avail. Ahead was an unidentified lake. There was no time to puzzle out his options. The choice was obvious. On a faltering engine, Steve pushed the plane's nose down and landed on the frozen lake. The plane slid for 100 yards before skidding to a stop close to shore.

The sun was fading fast and the temperature was dropping. Steve jumped out of the plane, walked around to the engine and examined it. But in the failing light, he couldn't find the problem. The wind whipped about him, howling in his ears, and he felt anxiety begin to curdle in his stomach. He could do nothing in the dark; he would have to wait until morning.

He climbed into the cabin of his plane, ate some tinned fruit and crackers and washed the food down with water from his canteen. Still shivering, he wedged himself between the seats and wrapped himself in a sleeping bag. Slowly, the shivering subsided, and his eyes felt heavy.

He awoke screaming, the nightmare of the crash in Fort Frances still fresh in his mind. Covered in sweat, he was panting heavily; he looked frantically around, wondering where he was. A flash of starlight through glass told him he was in his plane, and he remembered the engine stalling. He was just beginning to relax when he heard a rustle outside. He held his breath and listened to footsteps just below him. Something snorted and breathed raggedly. Then a wolf howled, and a chorus of howls joined the one as two, three and four more sang out. Steve grabbed his rifle and chambered a round, wondering if the wolves could get at him. Then, just as quickly as it started, the howling ceased. Another snort sounded, then footsteps again, this time leading away from the plane. He waited a few more minutes but heard nothing but the wind. He lay back, rifle clutched in his arms, staring at the ceiling of the cockpit.

When he awoke, it was daylight. He opened the door carefully, gun ready, surveying the ice and trees around him. On the snow were fresh tracks that looped in and around and under the airplane but no wolf in sight.

Gun in hand, he explored the tree line that surrounded the lake until he found a trail leading through the woods. Seeing no other alternative, he followed it. The snow was packed down, as if it was used frequently. Steve's eyes roamed the trees, searching for any sign of danger. He stopped and sniffed the air. The acrid smell of smoke tugged at his senses. He hiked up the trail until a structure loomed ahead. He approached the small wooden cabin cautiously; it looked as if it had been built recently.

Something yipped, and Steve spied a team of old, mangy dogs lounging outside the cabin. They began to howl and bark as Steve stepped closer. He stopped. The door to the cabin creaked open, and a Native emerged, dressed in furs from head to toe. He held out a hand, and the dogs fell silent.

He was middle aged, skinny but tall, and he had long, dark hair that fell about his face in dirty clumps. His face was pockmarked, his hands dirty and cracked. He said nothing, just stared at Steve.

Steve made sure his gun was pointed at the ground, holding it with just one hand.

"I'm lost," he shouted to the Native.

Still, the man said nothing.

"My plane quit. I had to land it at the lake. I need to get back to my base."

Still the Native said nothing, and Steve stood silently, awaiting a response.

"I have trapped in these woods for years. I know these parts well," the Native grumbled. "Where do you need to go?"

"A camp about 75 miles south of here," Steve told him.

The man nodded. "If you pay me, I can take you there by dogsled."

Steve smiled.

"I don't have any money with me, but I can pay you when we reach camp."

The man nodded again and gestured for Steve to follow. Inside, a stove glowed with a fire. Steve stood before it and felt his insides thaw. Within a half-hour, he was helping the man lash his provisions to a sled and hitch up his dogs. Then Steve took his place on the sled, and the dogs began to run.

They were not three hours from the cabin, when the dogs began to tire. Steve's new friend yelled at them and prodded them with a stick, but the dogs' tongues hung heavily from their mouths. They stopped to rest and feed the team, but when they finally got underway again, their pace was noticeably slower.

"They are old, my friend," the man grumbled in Steve's ear. "And they are not used to the extra weight. I had hoped that they still had their strength, but I see that they are tired. They will not make it to your camp."

He pulled on the reins, and the dogs gratefully halted. The Native reached into his pack and removed a pair of snowshoes.

"Take these and your provisions. Keep moving south until you reach a river, then turn to the east."

Steve choked on his anger, knowing he had several days of walking ahead of him with only a few days' rations. But he had no choice. He tied the snowshoes to his feet, slung his pack and rifle over his shoulder, checked his compass and began to tramp through the snow. He stopped and looked back. The Native was sitting on a rock with his dogs gathered around him, licking his hand. He looked forlorn. Steve shrugged and kept walking.

The wind blew hard at times, whipping up snow all around him. Other times the sun shone brightly off the snow, blinding him. He put an arm over his face and marched on, pushing branches aside and falling several times when his snowshoes snagged on saplings and tree roots. He walked until nightfall, stopping only when his body cried out for rest. When darkness came, he cut evergreen boughs to use as a blanket. In the morning, he began walking again at first light, struggling forward and pausing only to eat two small, unsatisfying meals. Just after noon, his big left toe went numb from the cold, and his hip throbbed mightily. He stopped and rubbed his blue-tinged toe until the feeling returned, but he could not sit and hold his toe forever. He reattached his snowshoe and trudged on. He collapsed just before nightfall, not bothering with branches; he just slept at the base of a tree. In the morning, his body ached, and his mind was foggy with fatigue and lack of food. He ate the last of his meager rations, drank the last of his water and set out. He limped through the snow, dragging his bad leg behind him. His beard was one frozen mass of snot and vapor, and his feet and hands tingled painfully from frostbite. Just before noon, he reached a frozen river and turned east. An hour later he heard noises—man-made noises. He hurried his pace. Just after 3:00 PM, he broke through the trees and found himself back at Cache Lake. He saw Al and Bernt and...his plane?

"What the hell is going on here?" Steve yelled in frustration. He shrugged off the helping hands of his co-workers and dashed for the plane, fumbling between the seats until his hand closed on his pipe. He hurriedly packed it with tobacco, lit it and sucked hard. His body sang in relief.

Later, over hot coffee and whiskey, Balchen recounted his story. "Saw your plane on my way back from Churchill," Bernt told him, topping off Steve's coffee mug. "Put down next to it. Al had a look and couldn't figure out why there wasn't any oil in it. We put some in and started 'er up. Al's got some flying time under his belt, so we figured we'd have him fly your plane back and look for you along the way. We're not in the air 10 minutes when flames, honest-to-god FLAMES, start shootin' out of your plane. Al sets it down, puts out the fire and finds a break in the oil line." Bernt shrugged his shoulders. "Al patches it up and we make it back here just fine."

One week later, Steve and Al were taking off from Cache Lake when their plane struck an ice hummock with a loud thump. Steve cursed and pushed the plane back to the ground. The undercarriage held, but barely. When Steve and Al checked the plane, they found that the undercarriage had cracked and was barely supporting its weight.

"Guess we'll have to walk," Steve grumped. He was not joking. The two lashed ropes to the wings of the Fokker and towed it back to camp. With Bernt gone to Churchill with the second plane, Steve and Al spent the next day pumping a handcar along the rail line to the rail repair shop at Pikwitonel, Manitoba. The effort strained and taxed Steve's back and shoulders, as he and Al pumped up and down, up and down. But the two made it to Pikwitonel, got the part and barely made it back.

"I'll never ride another goddamn train as long as I live," Steve groused as he fell into bed that night.

Steve and Bernt continued the same hectic pace, flying all day, every day, and on April 20, dropped off the last crewmen at Churchill. Bernt, Al and Steve celebrated by spending the next three days shivering in the cabins of their planes because they were forced down onto a frozen lake by a freak blizzard. When the weather finally broke, the three returned home. The next day, temperatures soared, and the ice began to melt.

In August, R.J. Jowsey contracted Western Canada Airways to move heavy machinery to the Sherritt-Gordon mine in northern Manitoba—30 tons altogether. Canada was slowly discovering that its foundation was a solid base of mineral wealth. Alberta was harvesting the oil that bubbled from the ground; in the Northwest Territories and northern Manitoba, men picked away at rock in search of diamonds; and the Canadian Shield was rich with nickel, zinc, gold and even glowed pink with the promise of uranium. The Québec Laurentians teemed with copper ore and lead. The mechanization of industry produced machines that made getting at minerals easier, but the machines were large and far too heavy to be hauled by land. Again the airplane took over where land vehicles failed.

Steve finished the contract on time and uneventfully. He flew as relaxed as ever, eyes half-closed, reclining in his seat and

Fred Stevenson delivers the *Winnipeg Evening Tribune* by airplane to mining camps in the Red Lake district. Newspapers across Canada sponsored several publicity stunts involving airplanes flown by some of Canada's most recognized pilots such as Stevenson and Wop May to cash in on the novelty of the flying machines.

letting the wind whip around him as he flew. At night, he slept hard without dreams. He almost never had nightmares now.

Steve continued hauling freight and men throughout the North during the cold winter of 1927 with no more accidents and no more breakdowns. Steve's confidence in his ability swelled, so much so that he approached the work with the same relaxed, happy-go-lucky attitude of his former self. Gone was the hard gruffness and the laser-like focus. Steve was where he belonged, and he loved it.

January 5, 1928, was a cold, clear day in The Pas, Manitoba, and Steve was putting a new Western Canada Airways Fokker through its paces. He taxied out on skis and pulled the plane off the ground, gently banking back and forth, climbing and descending with no trouble. The sun was bright, and the wind was cold, but bracing. Steve leaned back, leveled the plane off at 500 feet and smiled.

As he came in to land, the engine began to sputter and cough. Steve jerked upright and searched his instruments but found nothing. He looked out at the engine but saw no smoke, no fire. He pulled hard on the stick, as he overshot the landing strip and banked the plane left to come at it again. Suddenly, the engine revved mightily and the plane nosed down, plummeting to the earth.

"Frank!" his mind screamed. "Frank! What do I do? What do I do?"

But Frank wasn't there. And there was nothing he could do. This time, Steve didn't scream.

❧❖❧

In the summer of 1928, hundreds gathered to witness the opening of Winnipeg's first airport on the outskirts of the city. Dignitaries from the city of Winnipeg and surrounding rural communities flocked to the airfield to witness a truly historic moment.

A hush fell over the crowd as a man and woman, stooped with age but buoyed with pride, stepped up in front of the crowd. Steve had already been posthumously awarded the Harmon Trophy for Canada, one of the most prestigious awards in international civil aviation. He shared that international trophy with American aviator Charles Lindbergh. This day, the city of Winnipeg was ready to honor one of its own. Accepting handshakes from the gathered dignitaries, Fredrick J. Stevenson's parents unveiled a plaque set in marble at the entrance to the building to the gathered throng. It reads:

This aerodrome is named Stevenson Aerodrome in dedication to the late Captain F.J. Stevenson of Winnipeg. Canada's Premiere Commercial Pilot.

CHAPTER SIX

George William "Grant" McConachie

1909–1965

HE HAD DONE IT AGAIN.

Grant McConachie stood on the tarmac of Chicago's International Airport and reveled in his moment. He looked out over a gray, overcast sky and watched airplane after airplane plunk down onto the landing strip. The wind that whipped his hair was cool and smelled of gasoline. The roar of propellers drowned out the rush of wind. He smiled as he looked into his future. He had stared down disaster yet again, fought against apparently hopeless odds and triumphed.

The evidence to his ability stood behind him expectantly. Three men in long coats held their fedoras against their balding heads and squinted through the swirling air, waiting for him. Grant turned, flashed them a winning smile, and then walked towards the strangest looking aircraft on the field—the Fleet Freighter.

Grant climbed into the cockpit of the insect-like biplane and doffed his hat. He chuckled soundlessly as he proceeded with his preflight checklist, marveling at his good fortune. Not three months earlier, his company had lost three planes in one day, all in separate accidents. Only two had been insured. From the payouts on the two insured planes, he had purchased three Fleet Freighter aircraft, but Grant was informed by his local insurance broker that he would need executive permission on a policy for *any* plane he might buy in the future. Grant flew to Chicago with one of the Freighters to meet with the board of Aero Insurance in order to give his personal assurances that he would be more diligent with new his planes. With the new insurance policy folded in his pocket, Grant decided to give the board members a bit of a show as thanks for trusting him.

Satisfied that the checklist was complete, Grant jabbed the starter buttons with his finger. Both engines roared to life, then number one suddenly erupted in smoke as a large column of flame belched out of the engine and rolled towards him. He froze momentarily, but the heat from the engine fire melted the ice in his veins, and Grant grabbed his hat and scrambled out the rear door just as the flames reached the cockpit.

Grant didn't look back, he just kept running, his legs churning until he came face to face with the triumvirate of insurance salesmen who stood, mouths agape, watching their money go up in smoke. Grant turned and watched as the Freighter began to move, the second engine still running. The engine pulled the plane in an ever-increasing circle as it spun around and around, spewing flame. Sirens wailed in the distance as fire trucks screamed towards the plane. But they were still too far away, and the blazing Freighter was creeping slowly closer to a group of nearby planes, all fully fueled, all ready to burst into flame at the slightest hint of fire. Grant gritted his teeth anxiously and began to look around for a place to hide.

At that moment, the second engine succumbed to the flames, sputtered then died. The Freighter began to slow and creaked to a halt mere yards from the assembled wing of aircraft. The fire crews arrived and began to cover the plane in

Grant McConachie, who started flying a small bush operation out of Edmonton, became president of Canadian Pacific Airlines, Canada's second largest scheduled airline, in 1947.

fire-retardant foam. Men ran and shouted, trucks careened about and the air was thick with smoke.

Grant turned to the stunned board of Aero Insurance, his face smudged in soot and ash. He smiled.

"Any questions?" he asked.

George William McConachie was born in Hamilton, Ontario, on April 24, 1909. Shortly after his birth, his father William uprooted Grant and his mother, Elizabeth, and moved them to Edmonton, a booming town in central Alberta. William took a job as a district chief master mechanic with the railroad and moved his family into a three-bedroom house in the north of the city. As he grew, young Grant worked most weekends and after school, first with a paper route, in a lumberyard and then on nearby farms as a laborer. His tall stature and sinewy build made him a natural for sports, and he excelled at hockey, football and basketball.

Early on Grant showed signs of being an independent spirit and a visionary who possessed the determination to make his vision a reality. On one occasion when his parents were in Chicago for a vacation, Grant and a friend liberated the McConachie family car from the garage. Although his father had locked the garage door, hidden the car keys and removed and locked up the carburetor to ensure that his son couldn't get into trouble, Grant and Cam were determined. They removed the garage door from its hinges, found the keys and borrowed a carburetor from a neighbor.

For the week his parents were away, Grant knew freedom. He and Cam cruised the neighborhood, showing off to their friends and trying hard to impress the local girls. But the day before his parents returned, Grant was parking the car in the garage, when he noticed tire marks on the cement, marks that would surely give him away to his father. He could think of only one way to could avoid getting into trouble. That night, Grant and Cam packed their clothes, withdrew all the money in Grant's bank account and hopped a westbound train to Vancouver to join the Navy.

Unfortunately, the conductor of the train recognized Grant and sent word to his father. When the train pulled into Jasper, the conductor escorted both boys off the train and locked them in a storage room at the station until Grant's father arrived. Even though he was angry at his son, William McConachie listened instead to his growing boy argue for his freedom, against having to work after school and on weekends and against not being able to use the car. Instead of punishing Grant, William cut a deal with his son. If he passed his Grade 10 exams, he could make his own decisions about his life.

After passing his exams, Grant dropped out of school and took a job in Jasper wheeling ashes in a steam plant. But the hard, dirty work combined with the high cost of living soon chased him back to Edmonton where he re-enrolled in school. When he wasn't in school, Grant spent time at the nearby Edmonton airport, watching planes take off and land. He huddled in the nearby Royal Signals shack, listening to the radio calls of bush pilots, fascinated as their stories unfolded in terse "radio speak."

On graduating from high school, he enrolled at the University of Alberta and immediately fell into a routine, spending his days at classes in engineering at the University of Alberta and his afternoons and evenings working so he could spend his weekends flying. He took lessons at the Edmonton and Northern Alberta Aero Club under the tutelage of Jimmy Bell and soloed after only seven hours of instruction. He was a natural flyer, getting his pilot's license in March 1930, but he was also a rebel who continually violated the rules of the aero club. He was grounded twice for carrying passengers without a commercial pilot's license. On one occasion, he took the club's Pus Moth without permission and disappeared for four days. When he returned, the rumor was that he had flown a miner all the way to the United States, but it couldn't be proven. The fast-talking McConachie managed to avoid having his flying privileges revoked.

In November 1931, following a stint in Portland, Oregon, McConachie received his commercial pilot's license. But the need for pilots in Canada was small. With the country in the grip of the Great Depression, the government was no longer interested in such fanciful excesses as airmail or airfreight. Pilots stood in long unemployment lines with every other man in Canada, looking for any kind of work. The prairies, hit hard by drought, were a dustbowl that yielded smaller and smaller crops and withered animals. And so Grant jumped at the first pilot's job he was offered—in China.

The Chinese government wanted to start an air service and was promising upwards of $300 per month to skilled pilots. In times of war, however, the contract stipulated that Grant could be drafted to serve in the military. Still, the idea of flying overseas fascinated him, and he hopped a train to Vancouver to sign on with a proposed Chinese air service based out of Shanghai. While he was in Vancouver, McConachie stopped in to visit an uncle who changed the course of his life forever. Uncle Harry McConachie, his dad's brother, considered himself a shrewd businessman (others thought him a swindler) and, not wanting to see his favorite nephew stranded in a foreign country working lord only knows where, Harry proposed a radical idea.

"What if you and I started our own air service?" Harry asked Grant, as the two sat in Harry's opulent Vancouver hotel room. "I'll front the money, you take care of the flying."

"This won't make us rich, Uncle," Grant warned, thinking of the Depression.

"Good things come to those who wait, my boy," Harry replied with a soft smile.

Grant proved to be as shrewd in his business, and possibly more honorable, than his Uncle Harry. He purchased a used Fokker Universal in Edmonton and set to work immediately hauling fresh fish from Cold Lake to Bonnyville. He took jobs other pilots turned up their noses at, not only flying fish, but also fresh fruits and vegetables, which he would sell from his plane. It may have been dirty, smelly work, but for McConachie it was a chance to make money. Although his plane could only carry a maximum payload of 800 pounds, McConachie frequently hauled loads in excess of 1200 pounds. Within a few months, he made enough to repay his uncle for the cost of the plane.

When summer came, McConachie barnstormed, giving plane rides and putting on aerial displays at carnivals and fairs throughout northern Alberta. Within a year, his small company, Independent Airways, was operating three planes—another Fokker and a Pus Moth. Emboldened by his success, Grant concocted larger schemes that could further demonstrate the utility of his airplanes. One summer, he even persuaded a group of miners in the small mountain town of Robb to clear trees for an airstrip so that he could transport miners to and from the camp. The idea didn't pan out, but it was indicative of McConachie's vision for how airplanes could function. Each time he went aloft, his mind swam with ideas. He dreamed of flying into the most desolate regions of Canada with goods and supplies, of offering passenger service across the West, even expanding overseas to Hawaii, Russia and China! He saw a place for air transport and passenger service and worked tirelessly to achieve it.

Grant was also generous with his gift. In November 1932, an urgent call came into the Royal Signals hut at the Edmonton airport. The message described a terrible accident at a telegraph station in Pelican Rapids, 175 miles northeast of Edmonton. The small, isolated shack was manned by Frank and George Senz, and both had been horribly burned in an explosion caused by a leaking gas pipe. The brothers urgently needed medical attention and would likely not survive a trip by dog team.

The message came from a nearby trapper who had traveled nine miles to the next station to alert the authorities. But the rescue would be a daunting task. It was between flying seasons.

The ice on the lakes and rivers was just forming, too thin to support a plane, and the area around the telegraph station was heavily wooded with no clearings large enough for a plane to land. Three days passed before Edmonton officials found a pilot willing to take the risk. It was Grant McConachie.

He instructed the trapper to take the injured men to nearby Oboe Lake, 10 miles from the telegraph station. Grant thought that the lake's beach was large enough to land on. It was a long shot, so dangerous that the military would not send a doctor along to treat the brothers on-site. But it was their only chance.

When Grant and mechanic Chris Green arrived at Oboe Lake, McConachie realized just how dangerous the situation was. Grant had instructed the trapper to start a fire along the shore so Grant could use the smoke to judge the wind. But the trapper, buoyed by adrenaline, had ignited a massive bonfire that produced so much smoke it obscured Grant's view of the beach. Grant approached from an angle, with the wind at his back, the plane hovering just above stall speed. He skimmed along the shoreline until he reached an area of beach wide enough for the plane. Uttering a silent prayer, Grant pulled back on the throttles, cut the ignition and hauled back on the column, stalling the airplane. The Fokker coughed and sputtered, then smashed into the ground. The plane skidded and slewed, churning up sand in a frightening spray. A sudden ripping sound sent chills down Grant's spine. He looked down to see a thick tree root tearing through the skin of the plane right down the center. The plane slowed quickly to a halt. Grant wasted no time. He grabbed a bag of medical supplies and ran full tilt to where the two brothers and the trapper cowered in the trees.

"Aren't you a sight for sore eyes!" one of the brothers managed, jokingly of course, for both brothers' eyes were swollen shut. Their skin was charred and oozing, and Grant's nostrils detected the slightest scent of rot. He worked quickly, dressing and bandaging the brothers' burns as best he could while his mechanic, Chris Green, mended the torn fabric of the Fokker.

After bandaging the brothers and loading them into the plane, Grant realized he had another problem. He didn't have enough room for takeoff. Because the Fokker had no brakes on its wheels, Grant had no way to hold the aircraft in place while he revved the engine to full power. So Grant, Chris and the trapper hauled the plane back to the tree line and tied the tail to a stout tree trunk. Grant took his seat at the controls and revved the engine up to full power. The plane pulled and strained against the rope, but the tree didn't budge. Grant stuck his arm out the window and made a slicing motion. The trapper, standing behind the plane, raised his ax and severed the rope with one clean stroke. The Fokker lurched ahead, building up speed quickly, then soared into the air. Everyone sighed in relief as Grant pointed the plane towards Edmonton.

The mercy flight was astonishing, unparalleled in its bravery and ingenuity. But McConachie couldn't have foreseen the disaster that would befall him later that month. It was time to start flying fish again. One cold and foggy morning, as McConachie was preparing to take off from Edmonton, he and his new mechanic, "Limey" Green, went through the preflight checklist, started the plane and revved the engine. They were about to release the brakes when a tall, bespectacled man ran towards the plane. It was Grant's Uncle Harry, fresh off a train from Toronto, checking up on his nephew. Grant left the plane idling and hopped out to talk to his uncle.

"A little foggy to be flying, don't you think," Harry said by way of greeting.

"I can get above the fog just past St. Albert," Grant replied. "Should be able to clear it without a problem."

"You just be careful with my money," Harry told him pointedly, then laughed.

Grant clasped his shoulder affectionately.

As the two chatted on the airstrip, the props of the Fokker continued to swirl in the early morning fog. The tiny frozen particles cooled the temperature of the propeller blade, then stuck to it, slowly forming an invisible sheet of ice along its length. When Grant bid his uncle farewell and returned to the plane, he couldn't know what was about to happen.

His first clue was on takeoff. Although the throttles were pushed all the way in, his ground speed was negligible. His eyes flicked between the end of the runway and the speedometer. He was halfway down the airstrip now, and he had no room to stop. He was committed to takeoff. Pulling on the control column, he willed the plane into the air. It resisted for a moment, then grudgingly yielded and skipped off the ground.

But with no speed, the plane couldn't climb. Wheels mere feet from the ground, the engine hovering at stall speed, Grant was worried. He dodged the looming smokestacks of the nearby CN rail yards, pulling gently at the stick, trying to gain some altitude. A set of power lines came up suddenly right in front of him, but he still had no speed, no altitude. He pulled the control stick left and tried to bank away from the power lines, but it was a catastrophic choice. As the plane banked, the left wing dipped so low that it struck the ground with a sickening crunch. The impact with the ground caused the plane to cartwheel tail over nose. Limey yelled in terror, and Grant clutched his hands over his head, exhaling sharply as his body was battered by the impact. The plane rolled over and over, the sound of wrenching metal digging into his ears, and Grant wondered if he would feel the heat of the exploding gas tanks before he died.

But he felt no heat. The mangled Fokker flopped over and stopped in a farmer's field on the outskirts of Edmonton. Dazed, Grant pulled his arms away from his head and looked around. Limey sat beside him, staring straight up at the sky revealed by the torn roof of the cockpit, breathing heavily

although seemingly uninjured. Grant tried to wriggle out of his
seat but gasped in pain when he tried to move his legs. Looking
down, he saw that his left foot was bent at an unnatural angle.
It took him a moment to realize his ankle had snapped in two,
then he recoiled in horror at the sight of a metal rod sticking
out of his arm like an arrow.

Outside, the silence following the crash was replaced by
the clamoring of a crowd rushing to their aid. Doc Cameron,
the McConachie's family doctor who lived near the airfield and
had heard the crash from his home, crouched next to the
wreckage and passed in a bottle of whiskey, motioning for
Grant to drink up. By the time they pulled him free of the
wreckage, the liquor had kicked in, and Grant was too drunk to
mind the pain. At the hospital, x-rays showed that Grant's legs
were broken in 17 places. He also had several broken fingers,
ribs, two broken hips and a shattered kneecap.

"You'll be walking funny for a long, long time," Dr. Cameron
assured him.

The doctor was right. At the end of a two-month hospital
stay, Grant was walking funny, his left leg stiff from the recon-
struction of his shattered left knee. Not one to bow to circum-
stance, Grant took matters into his own hands. On one
occasion, he begged a group of drunken friends to jump on his
knee in order to loosen it up. The end result would have been
comical were it not so painful. He held his leg over the edge
of a table, and the knee did not give as expected when jumped
upon. Instead it acted as a lever, catapulting Grant across the
room. He endured several days of swelling and pain, but his leg
did loosen up considerably. A few months later, while lifting
barrels out of his plane, Grant felt his knee give way under the
weight of a barrel. He endured two more days of intense pain,
only to discover that his knee had loosened up almost entirely.

In February 1933, Grant was presented with another opportunity. Barney Phillips, a grizzled, street-smart prospector from

British Columbia, hired McConachie to fly him and his team to an abandoned gold mine. But the site was located in the Stikine Range, a granite spinal column of sharp peaks and ridges that ran from Alaska into northern British Columbia. Few men had ever ventured into the Stikine and returned alive. No airplane had ever penetrated its jagged tips.

"If we go down, there's no coming back," McConachie warned Phillips, as the two negotiated Grant's fee.

Phillips gave Grant a stony look. "The prospect of gold infects the mind of anyone who contemplates it. They'll do anything to get it. I'm willing to do anything to get it first."

Undaunted, McConachie and Phillips headed into the Stikine Range. Grant sweated the entire trip, slicing in between the dagger-like edges of the mountain range. The cold wind hammered his Pus Moth, tossing it around the sky like one of the millions of snowflakes that swirled around them. After hours of on-the-edge flying, Phillips shouted and gestured. Ahead lay their destination, Two Brothers Lake. Grant managed a perfect landing upon the purest blanket of snow he had ever seen, and also the deepest. As the Moth slowed, it sank up to its axle and would not budge. McConachie, Phillips and his team trampled a small runway in the snow with their snowshoes so Grant could take off again.

Upon returning to Edmonton, Grant came face to face again with his lifelong disciplinarian, Jimmy Bell, steward of the Edmonton and Northern Alberta Aero Flying Club. No sooner had Grant landed at the city's airfield than a creditor's tag was slapped on all his planes. The money had run out. Uncle Harry and his business partners no longer saw eye to eye on business matters. Independent Airways was bankrupt.

Grant begged and pleaded with the creditors, who grudgingly released one of the Fokkers so Grant could earn some money barnstorming to pay off the company's debt. Unfortunately, three weeks later, one of Independent's pilots crashed the Fokker. It was an inglorious end to an ambitious flying venture, but it left Grant in an even deeper hole. Phillips and his crew were expecting him to bring supplies to Two Brothers Lake, and Grant had no way to get them there.

Grant went to Vancouver and managed to convince a friend, Charlie Elliot, to fly his Junkers monoplane into the Stikine to pick up the miners. It was now two weeks past the date Grant was supposed meet the miners with supplies, and he was anxious. He and Elliott left Vancouver early one June morning, but were forced down hours later on Takla Lake because a rocker arm on the engine had lost a roller. It was a necessary repair, but they carried no replacement parts and had no way to get off Takla Lake.

Grant found a dugout canoe on the shore of the lake and tried to row his way to nearby Baker Lake for help. Even though Grant was a capable pilot, he couldn't paddle a canoe worth a damn. Not even halfway across the lake, he rolled the canoe for the third time. Sputtering water, soaked to the bone, Grant dragged the canoe back to the shore, despairing at his luck. Time was running out for the miners. If they didn't survive, if Grant didn't get back to meet them, he was finished as a pilot. One of the cardinal rules of a bush pilot was that you always went back for the crews you left.

Meanwhile, Elliott had formulated a plan. After five days of careful filing, he had drilled out the middle of a socket from his socket set, hoping it could replace the broken roller. It worked but was only a temporary fix that would not hold for long. Forced to return to Vancouver, Elliott dropped McConachie at Baker Lake and headed for home.

At Baker Lake, Grant dashed from plane to plane, begging pilots to fly him into the Stikine, but they were all either too busy or too intimidated by the geography. After three weeks of desperate pleading, Grant finally convinced Ken Dewar of Consolidated Mining and Smelting to fly him in. Grant was now six weeks overdue, and when the plane touched down at Two Brothers Lake, Grant was relieved to find all the miners alive, if only barely. They were shadows of their former selves, skeletons who could not walk unaided. Grant and Dewar loaded them all into the plane and flew them back to Vancouver for medical treatment.

A few days later, Phillips summoned Grant to his hospital bed. Grant explained the entire fiasco and fell silent, waiting for Phillips to yell himself hoarse.

"How would you like a job, son?" the old man asked.

Grant was thunderstruck.

"What kind of pills are they giving you?" he blurted.

But Phillips was quite lucid and wanted to know if Grant would help him start up his own airline. It would be a bush operation, servicing his miners as well as taking on other jobs. Grant would be in charge of the flying and Phillips in charge of the prospecting. Grant quickly agreed, and on that day, United Air Transport (UAT) was born.

Based out of Calgary, Alberta, the operation began with two Fokker aircraft purchased from a bankrupt air service company. With winter fast approaching, Grant found work flying fish, this time from Peter Pond Lake to Cheecham, Alberta. When he wasn't flying fish, McConachie was flying supplies to miners throughout western Canada. But the small Fokkers were limited in the amount of weight they could carry, limiting the amount of money they could make hauling freight. To address the problem, Grant purchased a Ford Trimotor plane, at the time one of the biggest aircraft in Canada. With its three engines, its ability to operate on skis or wheels and its enormous payload, the Ford helped Grant pull ahead in the airfreight business. From 1934 to 1935, United Air Transport hauled more than one million pounds of fish.

Grant's flying skill and determination made him a familiar face in the growing community of Alberta pilots. In May 1936,

Grant was preparing for barnstorming season when he received a proposition that landed him another aviation first. A rich oil tycoon named Wilkinson wanted to get from Calgary to Vancouver and wondered if it could be done by air. It had never been done before, but that didn't stop Grant from giving it a try. The press picked up on the story, issuing radio broadcasts, and a large crowd gathered in Vancouver to await the first-ever commercial flight across the Rockies.

Only hours out of Calgary, Grant was delayed because of ice build-up on the wings of the plane. He was scheduled to arrive in Vancouver in the early afternoon, but he didn't arrive until shortly after 6:00 PM, leading some radio stations to report that his plane had gone down in the mountains. But Grant and Wilkinson arrived in Vancouver to a hero's welcome. The mayor greeted McConachie under the mistaken notion that Grant was establishing a regular commercial air route between Calgary and Vancouver. When it became clear that this was not the case, Vancouver withdrew its courtesy and hospitality. Grant was left with a hotel bill so large he was forced to spend the summer barnstorming in northern British Columbia to pay it off. He did manage to return in time to marry his longtime romantic interest, Margaret MacLean, a nurse he had met while recovering from his horrific crash in November 1932.

In July 1936, determined to get its share of the airmail pie, UAT applied for one of the coveted airmail contracts offered by the government. With the Great Depression slowly abating, the government was looking for faster and cheaper ways to communicate with its citizens. While the train offered a speedy alternative, not enough rail lines existed to sufficiently service Canada' most remote regions, specifically the North.

UAT applied for a route between Fort St. John and Fort Nelson in northern British Columbia. The government sent out Postal Inspector Walter Hale to meet McConachie at Cooking Lake near Edmonton. The two were scheduled to fly the route together so that Hale could determine if UAT was up to the task. Along with several bags of mail, McConachie also loaded the plane with fresh eggs, fruit and other supplies to sell to northerners, both to make a few extra dollars and to make a good impression on Inspector Hale.

With the no-nonsense inspector buckled into his seat, McConachie steered the Fairchild FC2W2 out onto Cooking Lake. Unbeknownst to Grant, the ground crew had neglected to replace the plugs that kept water from collecting inside the airplane's floats. As the Fairchild roared along the surface of the lake, water pooled inside the floats, and the plane started sinking. Grant was too busy checking the oil temperature gauge to notice the problem.

"Uh, sir? I think we're sinking," Hale said in a rising voice.

Grant froze and stared out the window, seeing the plane slowly begin to settle below the waterline. The floats were already submerged.

"I do believe you're right, Inspector," said McConachie, as he pushed the throttles to the stops. The powerful engine of the Fairchild roared, pulling the plane's floats slowly back out of the water as Grant steered back to shore. Once the water was drained and the plugs replaced, the trip went off without a hitch. UAT landed the contract.

Over the next two years, UAT also landed airmail contracts from Edmonton to Whitehorse, from Vancouver to Fort St. John, and from Prince George to Fort St. John. The fleet of planes operated by UAT grew to 12, but UAT still wasn't profitable. The planes were too small, and the three-engine Ford had been retired years before because it couldn't take off or land on water. All of UAT's planes operated on floats or skis, and two months out of the year—November and April—no business could be done because the lakes were either just freezing or just melting and could not support the weight of the plane. McConachie persuaded Barney Phillips' son, also

named Barney, to direct the company towards wheeled aircraft, thereby raising the possibility of using larger planes to
carry larger loads, even human cargo. The company began
clearing airstrips all along its routes for use year-round by
wheeled planes and even dressed the pilots in snazzy blue
uniforms.

But the money didn't start to pour in overnight, and the
company was dangerously close to a financial crash landing.
Money was so tight that Grant could only afford to insure two
of the 12 planes in his fleet. On November 3, 1938, Grant was
struck with a heavy dose of bad luck when three of his planes
were destroyed. One burned up during repairs, a second sank
through thin ice, and the plane sent to retrieve the pilot who
had sunk through the ice got to his plane only to find that
a violent windstorm had flipped it upside down. Fortunately
for Grant, two of the three planes were the two that had been
insured. Grant used the insurance money to make a down payment on three Fleet Freighter aircraft, which were larger,
wheeled, oddly designed planes that he felt were the wave of
the future.

But the local broker of Aero Insurance was not willing to
insure UAT's planes without the expressed personal approval of
head office in Chicago. Grant made the trip himself and
explained his vision to the president, treasurer and actuary of
the insurance company. Within minutes of beginning his pres-
entation, Grant had the three hooked on his tales of wilderness
survival, of crashes, rescues and mercy flights and of opening
up Canada's Barren Lands to businesses. Rapt by his stories, the
board of Aero Insurance signed off on a policy for the three
new Fleet Freighters. Once he ensured the details had been
wired to Edmonton for processing, Grant invited Harvey, the
president, McIvor, the treasurer, and Freeman, the actuary of
Aero Insurance, out to the Chicago Airport for a demonstration
of the Freighter's capabilities.

The three men stood on the tarmac, horrified as one of the planes they had just insured burst into flame before their very eyes. Grant managed to escape just as the Freighter began careening wildly around the airstrip, threatening several other fully fueled planes parked nearby. Emergency crews managed to put the fire out, but not before UAT's new plane was completely destroyed. Fortunately, the insurance policy was in effect that day.

UAT changed its name to Yukon Southern Air Transport in March 1939 and continued its work, focusing on establishing air routes throughout British Columbia and Alberta and hauling mail and supplies. But the company was as deep in debt as ever, and when World War II broke out in Europe, the situation only became worse. Mines shut down all across the country as men enlisted in the army, thus depleting most of Yukon's clientele. Pilots became scarce because they were drafted into the Royal Canadian Air Force. It seemed to be only a matter of time before Yukon would join so many other airlines on the scrap heap of history.

But the Canadian government came to the rescue of Grant McConachie's little company in a backward way. Although dozens of tiny air companies had tried their hand at flying across Canada since the 1920s, the nation did not yet have a nationwide carrier that offered coast-to-coast service. The Canadian government, under Prime Minister William Lyon Mackenzie King, began to fear for the nation's sovereignty. The U.S. already had two national carriers, and the government was worried that those airlines would expand their services into Canada before long. In response, the government started Trans-Canada Airlines (TCA) with passenger service from one end of the country to the other.

But just as the government decided to throw its hat into the ring, a private concern also began work on the notion of a national airline. The Canadian Pacific Railway (CPR), which

Grant McConachie with new Lockheed aircraft delivered to Yukon Southern

operated most of the rail lines in Canada, quietly began buying up all the bush-flying companies it could find. In January 1941, CPR purchased Yukon Southern Air Transport and made its planes part of its fleet, which would later be named Canadian Pacific Airlines. Grant was hired to an executive position with the company as it fought against the government-sponsored TCA for the right to service the nation.

But in 1941, CPA was called into the service of the country. Japan had declared war by attacking Pearl Harbor and killing thousands of American sailors on December 7, 1941. The U.S. feared that Japan would also attack Alaska from an air base in the Aleutian Islands, but had no way to ship troops and tanks north to defend its territory. The Canadian and American governments agreed to build a road from Dawson Creek in northern British Columbia to Fairbanks, Alaska, to allow for the quick transport of forces north. Grant was asked to contribute to the aerial surveillance needed in order to find the best possible route. With Grant's help, 1600 miles of road were completed by October 1943. For his efforts in building the engineering marvel called the Alaska Highway, Grant McConachie was awarded the McKee Trophy for the advancement of aviation in Canada in 1945.

Grant's work on the highway, along with his attitude and determination, caught the attention of his supervisors. McConachie had a vision for transoceanic transport, an idea he had been sitting on since his days flying fish for Uncle Harry. CPA's bush routes were sucking funds from the company coffers that could be used to expand the airline to China, Russia, Europe, Hong Kong, even Australia. He persuaded CPA's senior vice-president, W.R. Neal, to abandon the bush routes to smaller air services. In 1946, Neal relented, lopping off several regional services in favor of CPA's main routes. That same year, Neal was made president, and against the guesses of everyone else in the company, over names such as Punch Dickins and Wop May, Grant became Neal's assistant. A year later, in 1947, the company was stunned again when Grant replaced Neal as president of CPA.

But the company was in a difficult position. By virtue of its position as the darling of the Canadian government, Trans-Canada Airlines got first dibs on any and all international routes. CPA could only service those areas that TCA was not

Grant McConachie sits in the cockpit of one of CPA's Boeing 707s on a demonstration flight nonstop from Seattle to Tokyo.

interested in servicing, but that didn't stop McConachie. In 1948, Grant traveled to Australia, and after weeks of intensive negotiations, he successfully obtained an operating permit to fly from Vancouver to Australia with a stop in Hawaii. Shortly afterwards, Grant negotiated a similar arrangement with U.S. General Douglas McCarthy, the head of the U.S. administration for occupied Japan, to secure a permit for a Vancouver–Tokyo route. He concluded similar agreements with governments of China and Hong Kong. The initial fares were exorbitant, and the cabins on the first few flights were practically empty, but Grant was not deterred. He recognized the need for international travel, and he knew it would work.

The contracts continued to roll in. By 1951, CPA was flying to Mexico City, Lima, Buenos Aires, Amsterdam, Lisbon and Madrid. The success was tinged with disaster. Between 1948 and 1951, CPA lost passenger planes in four separate accidents. When the first jet airliner debuted in September 1953, Grant promptly ordered three. The result was catastrophic. As the first Comet 1 jet took off from its factory for delivery to Canada, its rookie pilot crashed the plane on takeoff, killing the 11 people on board. The contract for the jet aircraft was canceled shortly afterwards. Other airlines' Comets began disappearing from the skies all over the world.

CPA, however, was making progress. It had signed a contract in 1950 to fly soldiers bound for the Korean War from Vancouver to Tokyo. In 1955, CPA became the second airline in the world, after Scandinavian Airlines, to fly over the North Pole on a flight from Vancouver to Amsterdam. McConachie's focus on service and expansion allowed his company to worm its way into and profit from markets that had previously been exclusively TCA's. In 1959, CPA began twice-weekly service to Italy from Montréal, and then to Honolulu from Winnipeg. CPA's finances slowly began to change course. In 1961, the company lost $7.6 million, but by 1965, CPA had *made* $7.2 million. As a result, in 1963, McConachie was named Canadian Businessman of the Year by a group of 40,000 New York businessmen. At its height, CPA was the seventh-largest airline in the world, its gray goose logo flying to countless exotic destinations. Still enamored with the notion of jet airplanes, McConachie slowly began to build more reliable jet aircraft into his fleet, such as the Bristol

Britannia and the Super DC-8, allowing his airline to operate faster than ever.

But success was wearing on McConachie. He flew all over the world to negotiate new deals, spending hardly any time at home. He was overweight and overworked. He had taken up ranching as a hobby some years earlier but still devoted most of his energies to CPA. Despite his seemingly undying enthusiasm and love for his career, it all caught up with him June 29, 1965. While in Los Angeles negotiating a lease for a DC-6B aircraft, Grant McConachie died of a heart attack in his Long Beach motel. He was only 56 years old.

In 1968, Margaret McConachie and her two sons, Bill and Don, were invited to a ceremony in Vancouver. Before snapping cameras and a gathered crowd, the young woman who had nursed the once-broken bush pilot back to health unveiled a sign on a new highway leading to Vancouver International Airport, now named "McConachie Way." A plaque dedicates the highway to the memory of Grant McConachie:

>   "…*whose contribution to Canadian aviation places him in the forefront of memory.*"

CHAPTER SEVEN

Colin S. "Jack" Caldwell
1895–1929

The engine stopped dead, the nose came up then dropped fast and the plane started to spin. One minute Jack Caldwell was making a level test flight at 1500 feet to measure the speed of the brand new Vickers Vedette V that had been entrusted to his care by the management of Canadian Vickers. It was a gloriously clear day in southern Québec, a warm, sunny day, perfect for flying, except for the strong wind that came up that afternoon when he took the Vedette on its first test flight, fresh out of the factory.

The plane was spinning, and Jack wasn't sure what had happened. But he knew he was in trouble. The engine could not be brought back to life. The nose dipped until the plane pointed straight down at the water. The aircraft rotated over and over. Jack jabbed the starter and worked the throttle, but got no response from the engine.

Fighting the G-forces that crushed him into his seat, Jack struggled to sit upright. The wind pulled at him as he fought his way to his feet in the open cockpit of the flying boat and managed to get a leg up on the seat. He didn't stop to think about what he was doing because if he did, he knew he'd die. The waters of the St. Lawrence River were rushing up to meet him as the plane plunged ever closer to its icy blueness. With a silent, lightning prayer, Jack squeezed his eyes shut and jumped.

The wind threw him into the sky, and he twisted and clawed at nothing but air. The ground spun crazily around him as he plummeted hundreds of feet per second towards the earth. Despite the tearing roar of the wind, he heard nothing but the lub-dub of his heartbeat in his ears. He'd never felt anything like it in his life. He was falling, just falling. He wasn't attached to any line, any harness, any kind of belt. He was free-falling quickly towards the earth.

Jack's heart drummed a steady tattoo in his ears; he groped around his chest for the cord. His pinky found it fluttering against his left breast, but in his haste to pull it, he lost it. His fingers chased it through the air, the handle skipping across his fingers. Just as he began to despair that it was too late, he managed to grab hold, and he pulled.

With the rustle of silk, followed by the most abrupt halt Jack had ever experienced in his life, the straps of the parachute sawed into his clothing. He grimaced in pain, grabbing hold of the straps, and felt the air whistle through his teeth. He looked up, and seeing the parachute fully deployed and braking his descent, he exhaled loudly.

He kicked his feet wildly, unsure what to do with them. He surveyed the horizon as he glided towards the earth and saw the ribbon of the St. Lawrence twist into the sun, His skin tingled, and he shivered with pure delight. He had never before experienced such a raw sensation of nothingness. Then he looked down, and his eyes bugged out as the waters of the St. Lawrence raced up towards him. He had no idea how to land. He braced himself, thrust his legs out in front of him and closed his eyes.

The water was cold, so cold that he gasped as he plunged down into it. He closed his mouth as his head went under and then kicked forcefully, scissoring his legs to get his head above water. As he broke the surface, he felt something tug at his arms, then pull him across the surface. The wind had caught his parachute and was dragging him across the surface of the water.

As he neared shore, Jack managed to wiggle out of his parachute harness and slosh towards land. He shivered despite the warm, summer day and collapsed on the ground, cradling his knees with his arms to stay warm. His legs shook as he recalled falling. It had been the most liberating few seconds of his life, as close as anyone could ever come to experiencing so much of…nothing. He wondered if he'd ever feel that way again.

❧✦❧

Colin S. Caldwell was born in Fort Payne, Alabama, on April 14, 1895, of Canadian parents who had moved there from Ontario. His father heard of low-cost farmland in Canada, and he moved his family to Lacombe, Alberta, when Jack was 12 years old. Jack grew up on a farm south of Edmonton, the city that would become the capital of the new province of Alberta. He became known as "Whistles" for the corduroy pants he wore that scratched and swished as he ran. As both he and the 20th century began to grow, Jack watched the automobile creep onto the Prairies as more and more families in Alberta invested in that peculiar form of transportation. The horseless buggy made its way to farms in the area in the form of tractors and other machines that eased the backbreaking labor of harvesting the wheat, oats and barley that grew throughout the Prairies.

His father had always used horses, but slowly invested in such devices, and Jack was exposed to the inner workings of these wondrous machines. He spent his weekends and evenings tinkering, face smudged with grease and oil as he helped his dad repair the equipment. He was fascinated that the pumping of pistons, spinning of gears and whirling of belts could produce enough power to move a car, truck or tractor. Not only did they ease the demands of manual labor and allow more work to be done in a day, but the smallest engine could produce enough power to outrun the fastest horse and haul more produce than the strongest ox. Powered travel was the wave of the future, and even as a child, Jack wondered just how far it would go.

Like most Canadians, Caldwell was drawn to the news coming out of World War I as the local newspapers carried stories of the harrowing trials of Punch Dickins and Wop May, both Alberta boys, cutting swaths of German planes out of the skies over France and Belgium. Although he was working in Lacombe as a mechanic, Caldwell felt the pull of armed service and a fascination with machines that could fly. In 1917, Caldwell enlisted in the Royal Flying Corps (RFC) and was stationed at Camp Borden in Ontario as a flight mechanic. He was responsible for maintaining the base's small contingent of training aircraft. The skills he had acquired working on cars and tractors translated easily into a fluency in aircraft mechanics. By 1918, the young Canadian who had enlisted as a corporal was promoted to the rank of sergeant.

In 1918, Germany surrendered to the Allies, and a flood of Canadian soldiers returned home looking for work. Many found employment or decided to continue their education or careers in the military, but those who had served in the RFC returned home to find no careers in flying. The Canadian government, too broke to maintain a peacetime air force, disbanded that military branch following the war. "Jack," as Caldwell had come to be called in the RFC for reasons that were never clear to him, was also discharged from the military, and he returned to Lacombe to work as a mechanic. Being exposed to flight, however, had left an indelible mark on Caldwell's spirit. The challenge of maintaining such sophisticated machinery tugged at him, and the idea of one day learning to fly made the repair of autos and farm machinery seem mundane. But the airplane was still a novelty on the domestic front, too expensive and too fanciful to be of any real worth. As well, the aircraft were not built to withstand the rigors of the Canadian wilderness, and for several years, both pilots and engineers languished in jobs that, compared to flying, held very little appeal.

In 1920, however, Jack lucked out. Although it lacked any working planes, the government decided to form the Canadian Air Force (CAF), and Jack was one of its first recruits. He was made a Flight Sergeant, given a refresher course at Camp Borden in Ontario and then made an Instructor, Aero Engines. Caldwell spent his days illuminating the minds of pilots and would-be aeromechanics, teaching them the intricate mechanics of powered flight and demonstrating how to repair and maintain the few engines that were available to Canada's fledgling air force.

During his time at Camp Borden, Caldwell befriended a young Québec native named Roméo Vachon. Both had served overseas and the two were given a difficult assignment at Camp Borden: rebuild four Curtiss JN-4 trainers on a tiny budget. Undaunted, Jack and Roméo tackled the challenge with gusto, cannibalizing parts from wrecked and discontinued aircraft, slowly fitting the used pieces together like a puzzle. By 1921, the CAF had four new planes, and Caldwell was awarded his Air Engineer's certificate. Jack further added to his resume by taking formal flight courses at the birthplace of powered flight, Dayton, Ohio. Not only could Jack fix planes, he could now fly them as well.

His experience as a mechanic and a pilot made him attractive to one particular private concern—Laurentide Air Service,

an organization in Québec. Having purchased several HS-2L
Flying Boats at the end of World War I, the air service had been
watching Québec and Ontario's northern forests for Laurentide
Pulp and Paper Company. LAS hired Caldwell and Vachon as
pilots and engineers when they were not working for the CAF
during the summer months.

But their steeds were awkward, miserable machines. Made
entirely from wood, the Flying Boat was aptly named. The massive, single-engine biplane could only take off and land on
water. The pilot sat just in front of the rear engine and passengers sat in a turret at the front of the plane with no protection
from the elements. On landing, crewmen had to leap onto the
wing of the aircraft to add weight to one side to help steer it
towards its mooring.

But Caldwell soon found himself busy with the service, flying four-and-a-half-hour shifts every day, with observers
sketching the terrain below from the front turret of the HS-2L.
He also kept watch for columns of smoke surging up from the
tree line, indicating a forest fire. Although the job was sometimes boring, Jack was happy to be airborne and working on
his beloved machines once again.

On September 2, 1922, Jack was charged with being the
engineer aboard La Vigilance, one of Laurentide Air Service's
Flying Boats, for a truly historic mission. Stuart Graham had
flown La Vigilance in 1919 on what was considered Canada's
first bush flight. Graham flew the boat from Halifax, Nova
Scotia, to Grand-Mère, Québec, for the St. Maurice Forestry
Protective Association, the Laurentide Air Service's pred-
ecessor company. Caldwell and Don Foss, the pilot, were to
fly the Curtiss HS-2L from the LAS base at Remi Lake to Lac
Pierre, drop off a shipment of gasoline and then return to
the base.

"Should be a walk in the park," Foss muttered to Caldwell,
as they prepared the plane for flight.

Because it had no wheels, pilots of the ungainly Curtiss HS-2L Flying Boat, like the one shown above, used large lakes to take off and land.

❧✺❧

The trip from Remi Lake to Lac Pierre took exactly 90 minutes. They dropped off the gasoline, refueled the plane and turned around. They were not 10 minutes in the air when the skies, which had been gray and cloudy, opened up. Both airmen were soaked to the skin as great sheets of rain crashed into their aircraft. Foss yelled to Caldwell 10 minutes later, pointing a thumb at a lake below. Jack nodded. Foss was going to land the plane until the storm cleared.

Taxiing to shore, both Foss and Caldwell shivered beneath a canopy of trees just off the shore. As Jack watched the rain lash the surface of the lake, unease crept into his veins, whispering at the corners of his consciousness, telling him that something wasn't quite right. He scanned the horizon, then scanned the shore of the lake, and it hit him.

"Don," Caldwell tugged at his pilot's dripping sleeve. "That lake's not big enough for takeoff."

Don nodded, chewing on his lip.

"I think we might be able to, once the weather clears," Don groaned. "If we can't, I guess it will be a walk through the *bush* for us."

When the rain stopped and laser-like beams of sunlight pierced the clouds, Don and Jack remounted their wooden steed. The engine started with a belch of smoke and a mighty roar as Don eased the plane as close to the shoreline as he could. Jack tiptoed out onto the wing of the plane, adding his weight to the right-hand side so that it could turn more easily. Once the plane was pointed straight down the lake, Jack hopped back into his front-row seat and watched the far tree line rush to meet him. He swallowed, realizing he'd be the first to know if the plane didn't make it into the air.

With the throttles pushed to the stops, *La Vigilance* was still sluggish. Waterlogged from the storm, she was heavier than usual and slow to accelerate. Although the situation looked hopeless, Don pulled back on the stick anyway. The plane groaned as it lifted into the air, trailing water behind it. But after climbing all of five feet, it stopped, begging for more speed to gain more altitude. Don yanked the stick to the left, praying he could find enough room to escape the clutch of the trees that surrounded them, but his turn was too steep. As *La Vigilance* came left, her enormous wing clipped the surface of the water. The rest of the plane followed in a nauseating cart-wheel. Jack only had time to duck into his turret before he felt something kick him in the back. Everything went black.

When he awoke, he wasn't sure how long he had been out, but he heard birds chirping and felt water dribbling up his nose. He opened his eyes suddenly, flinging his arms out to either side. He felt nothing at first, then grasped something hard and wet: wood. He raised himself gingerly and realized that he'd been thrown from his seat and had landed, oddly enough, on the wing of the aircraft. His head and left leg throbbed with pain, but he was able to work himself up to his knees and survey the situation.

Something floating on the water caught his attention, and he inhaled sharply. Don Foss floated face up in the water, still strapped into his seat. From where Jack was standing on the wing, he couldn't tell if Don was breathing. A bubbling noise reached Jack's ears, and the plane suddenly lurched beneath him. Gripping the wing with both hands, Jack scrambled along its length. Dropping down into the water beside Don, he pulled at his harness, fumbling with the buckle in the cold, numbing water. The belt came free, Jack slapped the fabric away and grabbed Foss under his arms, towing him away just as the bulk of the plane disappeared below the surface.

Don awoke halfway to shore, thrashing his head about as Jack kicked towards the beach.

"Don!" Jack screamed, batting away Foss' flailing arms. "It's okay! I gotcha!"

Don ceased his protests and allowed Jack to pull him to shore. Arms burning, legs cramping, Caldwell crawled dripping and shivering from the waters of the lake. Foss lurched out of the water as well, clutching the back of his head and squinting in pain. The two examined each other and, finding no serious injury, flopped onto the sand breathing heavily.

"No one can get to us, Don," Jack said, pointing at the lake. If Don couldn't take off, no other plane in the LAS fleet would be able to either.

"Guess we walk," Foss shrugged, standing and offering Jack a hand up.

The remains of *La Vigilance* at Foss Lake following Jack Caldwell's September 1922 crash. Abandoned by Laurentide Air Service after the crash, the plane slowly began to settle into the silt of the lake, eventually slipping completely beneath the surface. In the late 1960s, Don Campbell, a businessman out of Kapuskasing, discovered the plane. The federal government, upon learning of the plane's resting place, decided to salvage it. When the operation to remove the plane from the lake began, it was known only that the plane was a Curtiss HS-2L, the last one known to exist in Canada. Only after salvaging began was it determined that it was in fact, *La Vigilance*, the plane that took part in the first-ever bush flight in Canada. The remains of the craft that could be salvaged were shipped to the Canada Aviation Museum, where it was put on display in 1986.

It took them all night to reach civilization. The night air was cold, even colder for the two flyers who were soaked to the skin. They followed the Groundhog River, staying along its shore, eyes scouring the surrounding bush for signs of human habitation or danger. Crickets played their eerie violins as the two stumbled through the trees in the dark, tripping on rocks and roots as they walked. Ghostly owls flew overhead and on one occasion, Jack swore as a flight of bats bombarded them. Their stomachs cried out in hunger, but all they had was the water from the river. Early the next morning, with the sun two hours old, they crashed through the trees into a clearing and came upon a cabin. A trapper, sitting on a log outside the cabin and whittling at a chunk of wood, greeted the two warily, but extended his hospitality once he heard of their plight. The next day, when the two airmen had sufficiently recovered their energy stores with wild game and whiskey, the trapper led them another few miles to the nearby rail stop at Fauquier, where they caught a train home.

Jack continued to fly for the rest of the season, even lending his skills and problem-solving ability to fellow pilots. Returning to Remi Lake from Moose Factory late one evening, Caldwell and his engineer flew over a lake and noticed one of the LAS's planes parked square in the middle of the lake. Deciding that no pilot would deliberately leave his plane in such a place, Jack circled the body of water and spied two small white dots jumping up and down on shore, waving frantically. Recognizing the two pilots as fellow LAS servicemen, Jack concluded the two had run into some sort of engine trouble, but with their plane blocking the landing path, Jack could do little to help them. With daylight waning, and the first hints of orange and purple beginning to kiss the sky, he was forced to head back to base.

The next morning, Jack took off once more, heading back to the lake. Swooping around its south shore, he saw the two men jumping up and down to get his attention. He also saw the words "drop gas" stomped into the muddy beach of the lake. Waggling his wings in acknowledgment, Caldwell returned to base. With the help of the crew, he filled five, five-gallon cans with gasoline and loaded them into his plane. Flying as low as he dared, Jack's engineer pushed the canisters overboard and into the lake. As the last can splashed down and Jack pulled back on the stick for altitude, he was rewarded with the site of a naked white backside diving into the lake.

Two hours after Jack returned, the two stranded men landed at Remi Lake. Two of the five cans had survived the impact with the water, giving the crew just enough fuel to get back to base.

"I think I speak for all of us when I say we're glad you guys are back, but the less I see of you the better," Jack laughed, when the men came to thank him. The two blushed and laughed, too.

In 1924, a new opportunity surfaced with his employer, LAS, but for a different purpose. Northern Québec was bursting, much like the rest of Canada, with untapped mineral wealth. At the tiny settlement of Rouyn-Noranda, a significant gold strike had been made, and a tide of miners and prospectors flocked to the region. Jumping at the chance to make a few bucks, LAS established the first-ever scheduled passenger air service in Canada, agreeing to fly anyone and anything to anywhere in northern Québec, provided there was a lake nearby.

That summer, Jack flew from one crazy situation to another. So many of the prospectors, who lived off the land, hadn't bathed for weeks and were often forced to hunt down their own food, turned white with fear when faced with the prospect of flying. They sat rigid in the turret of the aircraft, gripping the sides as hard as they could and watching the northern forests of Québec slide beneath them. Some were quiet with fear; others were agitated and talkative. Some sat perfectly still, and others drank heavily.

Early that summer, two miners approached Jack. They were well into their cups and asked to be flown to Rouyn-Noranda. They paid for the flight up front, so Jack saw little reason to turn down their offer. After loading their gear into the cargo hold, Caldwell took off. Jack watched as both men took turns reaching into their vests, bending forward and dipping below the edge of the turret then sitting upright. Jack's suspicions were confirmed when an empty bottle of whiskey was tossed into the air, nearly striking him in the head.

Suddenly, one of the miners lurched to his feet, slapping his friend's shoulder and gesturing to him with closed fists. Jack's skin sizzled with fear as the other man also rose, and with great difficulty, threw a punch. The two men were fighting! In an open cockpit, at 5000 feet!

Unsure what to do, Jack watched as the two staggered back and forth, pushing and clawing at one another. Just as one of them was close to being thrown over the edge, the aircraft hit a sudden downdraft, forcing the plane down hundreds of feet in seconds. Both men turned rigid with panic and quickly sat down, gripping their seats with all their strength. But Jack's laughter quickly turned to consternation when the plane landed. Both had succumbed to their liquor, too sick to hold in their stomach contents or stay awake. Jack had to carry both to shore and then clean out his passengers' seat.

Later that summer, while taking off from Rouyn, Jack wondered why he was having so much trouble keeping the plane level during flight. He had no passengers, no cargo, and was returning to the LAS base at Lake Temiscaming to check on any new schedules for the day. On landing, Jack asked several mechanics to help him find the root of the problem. One of the mechanics whistled from the rear of the plane, and Jack went to investigate.

"Looks like you had a passenger after all, Jack," the man laughed. Peering into the cargo hold, Jack came face to face with a very cold, very scared miner bundled into the rear of the plane. The man had wanted to return home to see his family, but did not have the money to pay for the flight. Instead, he sneaked aboard and spent a terror-filled hour airborne. He was the first-ever airplane stowaway in Canada.

In the winter of 1925, Jack took part in another unique flight enterprise. He was hired as the pilot for a plane being shipped out to sea on board the *S.S. Eagle* for the annual Newfoundland seal hunt. The simple idea was ingenious for its time: the plane would fly over the icepack, looking for the main seal herd, then return to the ship and direct the fleet towards its location.

The sealers, however, were not as eager to abandon their time-honored methods of guessing in favor of this new-fangled technology. The captain of the *Eagle* believed their intuition and experience would always trump progress, and it was with sadness that he ordered the Avro lowered to the ice in March 1925. Convincing the captain to keep the smokestacks of the *Eagle* spewing black smoke as a beacon, Jack soared up into the air, and within minutes, located the trailing edge of the herd. As it turned out, the fleet was headed in the opposite direction. So on his return to the ship, the fleet reversed its course, and within two days, had reached the hundreds of thousands of seals packed together on the spring ice off Canada's East Coast.

The sealers made a record catch that year and every year for the next three years, as Jack lent himself to the fleet until 1929. In 1927, because of Jack's advanced scouting, several of the ships filled their holds, returned to shore and headed back out for a second catch.

In June 1925, flying under contract for Laurentide Air Service, James Scott-Williams and Caldwell were hired by an American mining syndicate, the Detroit Mining Co., to fly a Vickers Viking IV aircraft into northern BC and the Yukon.

The two men were given the task of transporting a team of five geologists and prospectors to points throughout the North.

The Vickers was shipped from Montréal, Québec, to Prince Rupert, British Columbia, by rail and assembled. The rest of the summer was a whirl of fatigue and rushing wind as Caldwell and Scott-Williams logged 95 hours of flying time and 8000 miles total distance, successfully transporting their charges to uncharted points throughout the North with no mechanical problems or flying mishaps. They braved turbulent weather, wild animals and ferocious insects that tore away whole chunks of skin in a single bite as the pilots flew into regions of Canada that had rarely seen a human footstep, let alone an airplane. At the end of the summer, Jack Caldwell's reputation as a reliable, resourceful pilot and mechanic broke out across the flying community.

That earned reputation led to one of the strangest adventures of his life the next year. The Vickers Viking IV that Caldwell and Scott had flown the previous summer was purchased by a group of investors in Calgary called Northern Syndicate Ltd. The investors of Northern Syndicate had fallen under the spell of a grizzled old prospector's fantastic story that sounded too good to be true. The man had apparently struck gold in the Northwest Territories, a strike so large it could make all its investors rich. He had returned to Calgary because he lacked the equipment to excavate the gold, but showed the gathered group of businessmen a fistful of gold ore that he claimed came from the mine. He stated that he had carved the symbol of a cross into the brush surrounding the strike as a way to find it again and had left his Native wife to guard it. All he needed was a pilot and equipment, and he would willingly take them to the strike. The Northern Syndicate investors, listening to their wallets instead of their good sense, agreed and paid the prospector a substantial sum for the information.

Two days later, while celebrating his newfound wealth, that same prospector made the rounds of the taverns in Calgary. While indulging his thirst at one particular dive, the man became embroiled in an argument that escalated into a fistfight. In the heat of the moment, one of the bar's patrons grabbed a beer bottle and smashed it over the prospector's head, knocking him unconscious.

Although he awoke soon afterwards and did not suffer any permanent physical injury, his memory was badly affected by the incident. Try as he might, the man could not recall the location of the mine. Even under the most rigorous questioning, the prospector claimed to *know* of a mine, just not where it was...exactly.

Based on the information they had, which was sketchy at best, the investors of Northern Syndicate decided to proceed. After hiring Jack as chief pilot and Irenée "Pete" Vachon, the brother of Jack's service buddy Roméo Vachon, as air engineer, they shipped the Vickers by rail to Lac La Biche and assembled it. On June 22, Caldwell and Vachon set off for Fort Fitzgerald, where the party of prospectors awaited them. After ferrying the prospectors to the camp at a lake in the NWT that would later be dubbed Lake Caldwell, Jack, Pete and the rest of the party spent the remainder of the summer scouring the bush for the outline of a cross. For the entire month of July, whenever the weather was good, Jack and Pete took to the sky for as long as fuel and daylight would allow, but they ultimately found nothing. Any cross cut into the bush had long since grown over, and they could find no sign of any Native wife guarding any secret gold strike. In late August, with ice beginning to form on the waters throughout the North, Caldwell and Vachon flew the Viking out of the Northwest Territories to the RCAF base at High River where they left it.

Over the next three years, Jack kept busy flying with as many different organizations as possible. He spent his late

Jack Caldwell posing beside his airplane

winters and early springs with the sealing fleet on the Atlantic
Coast, scouring the icepack for signs of the main herd. He flew
airmail from Ottawa to Montréal and Rimouski for Canadian
Transcontinental Airways with his longtime buddy from Camp
Borden, Roméo Vachon. In 1928, he was hired as a test pilot
for Canadian Vickers in Montréal, but still kept up his sealing
and airmail responsibilities. As a pilot and engineer he was in
high demand, and Canadian Vickers recognized his skill. They
paid him well to put their new models through their paces,
listening closely as Jack suggested changes to the aircraft that
would make them more efficient, more useful and more reliable in the changing northern landscape. Punch Dickins, Wop
May and Doc Oaks were tearing the country apart with their
planes, charting previously unmapped territories, and if they
were to perform their jobs well, they needed reliable aircraft.

On May 17, 1929, Jack achieved another first in Canadian
aviation. On a test flight of a Vickers Vidette, the plane suddenly went into a spin, a spin Jack could not correct despite
all his flying and engineering experience and skill. With the
waters of the St. Lawrence River looming larger and larger
before him, a situation that would have spelled sure death for
any other pilot, Jack decided to put one of the world's newest
inventions to good use. Diving out of the doomed aircraft just
500 feet above the river, Jack pulled the ripcord on his parachute, becoming the first Canadian civilian pilot to save his life
this way.

But nothing could save Jack only a month later. Although
he was scheduled to take the day off on June 20, 1929, Jack
was summoned to work by the brass at Vickers to take a senior Vickers' employee and another passenger for a quick
spin around Montréal. He kissed Marion, his wife of a year and
a half, goodbye as he walked out the door and told her he'd
be home as soon as possible, as she was expecting their first
child in a few weeks.

It was hot and hazy that day in the air above Montréal, and visibility was somewhat restricted as Caldwell demonstrated the new Fokker Super Universal monoplane recently built at Vickers under license. The two passengers were Mr. Jarvis and Dr. Morris. It was partly because of that haze that Jack didn't see the electrical wire strung across the St. Lawrence River. The wire had been hung just that morning and was not known to any pilots based out of Montréal.

The wire tore through the thin metal of the Fokker's wing, shearing it away from the body of the aircraft. Jack came free of the plane and began to fall. The wind rustled his clothes and whipped his hair as he fell hundreds of feet. The feeling of weightlessness, of disconnectedness, was overshadowed by the absolute certainty of his death. He was falling from the sky to the ground below, and there was nothing he could do about it.

All three aboard perished in the crash. Jack Caldwell's body was found four days later.

~✺~

CHAPTER EIGHT

Maxwell William Ward

1921–

JULY 1946

The first time the plane flew over the baseball diamond, the players stopped their game to look up. An airplane was no longer a strange sight in the skies over northern Alberta, but it was strange to see one fly so low. It passed overhead, barely 100 feet off the ground, kicking up dust, grass clippings and leaves in its wake as it buzzed the motley collection of ballplayers. Squinting in the afternoon sun, the players could barely make out a goggled man at the controls of the open cockpit, but he was waving frantically at them.

They looked at one another, shrugging their shoulders, mystified at what the flyboy could possibly want. The plane tipped on its right wing and banked, reversing its course and buzzing the field again. The man in the plane was waving with two hands now, making a wild parting motion at the players below. He flew over the field again and turned once more, and this time, he began to descend.

The players, faced with a plane heading straight for them, finally clued in—the pilot wanted them to move so he could land. They scattered slowly at first, and then began moving more quickly as the plane dropped lower and lower. Pointing its nose at the outfield, the plane bounced once on the field, then settled and slowed. When it reached left field, it came to a stop. The frenetic buzz of the plane's spinning propeller ceased as the pilot cut the engine.

The players stood where they had stopped to watch. They waited, but nothing happened. Then a head appeared from the open cockpit, followed by a body. The arms were clutching something large and round. Closer inspection revealed it to be a 10-gallon barrel. The man waved at the players, this time more gently. Three of the players trotted over, annoyed looks on their faces.

"Hey there, fellas," the flyboy said in a friendly voice, flashing a smile that revealed a wide row of white teeth. "Just need a minute here, and then I'll be out of your way."

"What seems to be the problem, sir?" one of the ballplayers asked.

"Oh, nothing's wrong. Just need to gas up my plane. Ain't she a beauty?" The pilot smiled again, slapping the side of the biplane.

The players' eyes bulged. "You mean you've been flying with that drum of gasoline with you in the plane?" he asked.

"You bet!" the man said, unscrewing the cap to the fuel tank on the plane and beginning to pour the fuel in. "Had it between my legs the whole time. Got into Fort McMurray last night on fumes, so I figured I should take a little extra along with me just in case. This plane's a good one, but she's a bit short on range."

"Isn't that a little dangerous?" another player asked, noticeably shying away from the plane.

"If I crashed, it sure as hell would be. Imagine going down with 10 gallons of fuel right under your keester!" The pilot laughed, jiggling the barrel as he sloshed the last of the fuel into the plane. When it was empty, he tossed it back into the plane and reached out to shake the players' hands. "It was a pleasure to meet you guys. My name is Max Ward," he said, smiling again. He hadn't stopped smiling the whole time he was on the ground. "I was just on my way to Edmonton to get this little plane serviced and see my wife and daughter. I appreciate you letting me interrupt your game."

"Who do you fly for?" the first player asked, tugging at his ball cap.

"Well, truthfully, I don't really know," Ward said. "I've been flying with this fellow, Jack Moar, for a few months now, and this is our plane, but I just don't think it's the way to go. Being up there has given me a lot of time to think about things, and I think maybe it's time I branched out on my own."

His smile, if possible, became even wider when he said it.

"You guys keep your ears to the ground over the next while. I imagine you'll hear the name Max Ward again. And I hope it won't be my obituary."

He cackled, thanked the men again and hopped back into the biplane. The engine roared as it came to life, and within moments, the aircraft zoomed back into the air with Ward waving to the players below as he disappeared into the sky. The players straggled back to the infield to resume their game.

"Who was that?" the shortstop asked.

"Just some nut," one of the players replied. "Let's play ball!"

⚜

Maxwell William Ward was born in Edmonton, Alberta, on November 22, 1921. More so than most boys his age, Max was fascinated with flying. By the time he was a teenager, the airplane was a familiar sight in the skies over Edmonton, and a new breed of pioneer had emerged from the wreckage of World War I: the bush pilot. Men of exceptional bravery, skill and ability flew their rickety steeds deep into the wilds of

Canada's North, delivering supplies, machinery, food and medicine to people in remote camps and settlements. They mapped previously unexplored territories, rivers, streams and lakes and pried open the isolation that dominated the northern reaches. Names such as Wop May and Punch Dickins were on the lips of every Edmonton resident as these unflappable few proved the utility of their flying machines with stunning, previously unheard-of feats.

Max heard the stories and was captivated by them. He spent his free time at Edmonton's Municipal Airport, walking in and around the wood-and-fabric aircraft that landed there. At home, he carved toy airplanes from boxes he got at a nearby factory and raced along the streets beside his home, holding the planes aloft into the wind and making *vroom* noises as he teetered along the sidewalk. He never doubted that he wanted to fly, and when he turned 18, he set out to learn.

The best place to learn at the time was in the Canadian Air Force (CAF). When Max came of age to enlist, Canada was already embroiled in World War II. The army of Adolf Hitler had swept through Poland, Holland and France and held all of Eastern Europe in the fascist grasp of their fanatical leader. The Luftwaffe hammered the British from the skies, dropping thousands of bombs on London, Manchester and Newcastle. British Spitfires and Hawker Hurricanes took to the skies to valiantly defend the British homeland against attack, joining the Battle of Britain with great ferocity that soon decimated the ranks of the German air force. The toll was just as high for the Allies, and more men were needed.

The first time Ward applied to the air force, he was informed he could only be made a gunner…maybe. When he returned three months later, the CAF, having realized the number of bodies it would need to fuel the war effort, snapped him up and taught him to fly. He and his fellow recruits were sent to Edmonton, then High River for flight training. Although grateful for the chance to learn to fly, following orders had never been Max's strong suit. He continually ran afoul of his commanders, flying lower than regulations allowed because he was convinced that his superiors would never find out. But they always did. On one occasion, Max planned to meet his high school sweetheart, Marjorie, in Calgary to spend a weekend together. But Max was "gated," confined to the base at Claresholm, as punishment for his latest flying stunt. Looking back on the experience, both Max and Marjorie laugh about it, although at the time she was decidedly unamused by his sometimes reckless antics.

Upon receiving his wings in November 1941, Max was shattered to learn that he was considered so talented a pilot that the CAF was unwilling to risk his life overseas. He and one other pilot from his class were informed that they were being posted to Trenton, Ontario, to be trained as instructors. They would not see action overseas.

Max was heartbroken. He had so wanted to fly in the war that he cried that day in his bunk. But with the quality that would define the rest of his career, he took what was given to him and did the best he could with it. The next best thing he could do was marry Marjorie, which he did.

Ward was posted to Moncton, New Brunswick, to teach bombing and gunnery, and he developed a reputation as a strict, demanding instructor. He recognized his students' situation and felt responsible for their well-being. They needed to be well prepared if they were to survive the skies over Europe. Pussyfooting about their training would do them more harm than good. Max was firm when he had to be but glowing in praise when deserved.

The constant instruction and flying also helped hone Max's flying skills. During one training flight with two aircraft, Max gave the order for the two planes to form up on one another. Although Max's plane executed the formation perfectly, Max was shocked to see his wingman hurtling towards him. With a cool that surprised even him, Max took control of the Anson aircraft and tried to bank away from the incoming plane. The ensuing midair collision ripped the wing from Max's trainer. The plane was severely crippled, but he was able to land successfully. The same could not be said for the offending plane. Both men on board perished in the resulting crash. An official inquiry was unable to determine what had caused the incident.

Max left the air force in 1945 with 2800 hours of flying time under his belt and a specific goal—to be a bush pilot. The industry still needed pilots with the skill and flexibility to survive in the bush. Canada's North was bursting with minerals and oil, and in many cases, the airplane was the quickest, most efficient way to get supplies from place to place. Ward hooked up with Jack Moar, a veteran bush pilot in Yellowknife who had a solid skill set and a rather indifferent attitude towards his work. Moar was able to find two aircraft for their upstart business out of Yellowknife, Northwest Territories: a Cessna T-50 Crane and a Tiger Moth biplane. It took almost a year to get the business up and running, but in the spring of 1946, Max made his first bush flight. He and Moar were charged with delivering a load of surplus pipe to a nearby camp at Mills Lake. And on this first trip, Ward learned that bush flying was going to be unlike anything he had ever done in the air force.

When the two men reached their destination, Moar gestured to a dirty, muddy strip of land winding through the bush.

"Put 'er down there," Moar pointed.

"I'm pretty sure we can't land there, Jack," Ward mused. "It looks way too small, way too muddy to set down safely."

"Well if you won't put 'er down, I will," Moar harrumphed, taking control of the aircraft. Moar got the plane down all right, but he also sank it into the mud and shattered one of the Crane's propeller blades.

"Nice work," Ward said sarcastically.

Moar did not respond, but angrily exited the plane to examine their predicament.

It took several days of work to free the plane from the mud. The men were able to lay down stiff planks of wood on top of the mud to provide the plane a taxiway. They even managed to build a temporary bridge over a ravine that blocked their "runway." Max then shaved down the good blade of the propeller to match the blade that had been damaged during landing. Despite the mud and the broken prop, Max was able to get the plane into the air, then headed to Yellowknife for a replacement propeller and back to Mills Lake to pick up Moar. By the time he returned, the landing strip was dry enough to support the weight of the plane.

A less committed man might have turned his back on the entire idea of bush flying at that moment. It was dirty, messy, hard work with myriad unforeseeable dangers. But Max discovered, as he soared into the late afternoon skies, that he couldn't remember a time when he'd been happier.

The partnership with Moar did not last past the summer. Months later, Max took on the task of flying the Tiger Moth to Edmonton for maintenance. The tiny biplane was a good aircraft, but had poor range, requiring refueling every 130 miles. On the way to Edmonton, Ward was forced to interrupt a baseball game in Athabasca so he could refuel his plane from a 10-gallon drum he carried with him in the cockpit. The players thought him quite crazy, and to a certain extent they were right. Max came to a decision during that trip to Edmonton. He was ready to go it alone. He would start his own flying business in Yellowknife.

But business got off to a rocky start. Borrowing enough money for a down payment, Max traveled by train to Malton, Ontario, just outside Toronto, where he purchased a Fox Moth airplane from deHavilland Aviation. The diminutive biplane could carry 500 pounds of freight or three passengers, and

Max Ward with his Fox Moth in 1947

Ward thought it would suit his one-man enterprise. Beaming with pride at his newest acquisition, Ward took off for home. When he landed at an airstrip in Kenora, Ontario, for the evening, he did not know that the runway was being graded with gravel. The work crew had left a pile of it right in the center of the tarmac. Had Ward landed to the left or right of where he came down, he could have landed without incident. As it was, when Ward touched down, the plane ran smack into the gravel pile. The force of the abrupt landing propelled his face straight into the dash, breaking his nose along with his brand new plane.

It took five weeks to repair the Fox Moth and to also be approved to operate the plane on floats in the summer. When he returned to Yellowknife, Max took out an ad in a local paper announcing that Polaris Charter Co. Ltd. was open for business. He got his first charter within weeks and was soon busy flying miners and prospectors throughout the North. He was a one-man business, making his own bookings, flying and maintaining his biplane. He kept up a hectic pace, sleeping when he could, flying whenever possible.

But as he'd learned on his first bush flight, aviation in the North could be dangerous and challenging. While flying a gentlemen to nearby Arsenault Lake, the engine on the Moth suddenly quit. Keeping his cool, Ward was able to bring the plane to a controlled stop on the surface of the lake without incurring any damage or injury. When he checked the oil level in the engine, he was shocked to discover it was dry. Apparently someone's parka had caught on the spigot that drained the oil from the engine and opened it. The Fox had leaked oil the entire trip. It would need a whole new engine, a challenging fix in the middle of nowhere.

Challenging, but not impossible. Ward was no quitter, and he wasn't about to quit now. He hiked several miles to a nearby drilling camp, where he was able to flag down a Canadian Pacific Airlines plane for a ride back to Yellowknife. He wired deHavilland for a new engine on credit and traveled by train to Edmonton to take delivery. When the waters in the North froze in early autumn, Ward hitched a ride with another pilot, Garth Horricks of the Uscan Engineering Company, to the spot he had ditched his biplane. Over the next week, Ward awoke every morning and walked four miles from the mining camp where he was staying to where the Fox Moth waited. The work took several days of constant effort and an eight-mile round trip on foot each day, but the new engine started on the third try. Shaking his head the whole way home, Max headed back to Yellowknife where new troubles awaited him.

Like most industries in postwar Canada, the airline industry was tightly regulated. Max didn't know it, but no air service could operate without having first obtained a commercial air license from the government. Ward discovered this the hard way while loading his plane in Yellowknife. Two members of the Air Transport Board (ATB), infamous Québec flyer, Roméo Vachon, and Dan McLean, approached him at his dock at the Yellowknife airfield.

"Excuse me, sir," said one of the two well-dressed men who approached him. "Do you have a permit to operate a commercial airline?"

"Hell, no," said Ward. "Do I need one?"

The two from Ottawa ordered Max to stop his flights until such time as he could get a permit of his own, but they also provided him with a possible solution. A flyer in town by the name of George Pigeon had such a permit. If Ward partnered with Pigeon, his business could continue. Reluctantly, Max sought out Pigeon and the two formed Yellowknife Airways Ltd.

George brought two more planes to the company, a Stinson Station Wagon and a Piper Supercruiser, so the company could do even more business. Pigeon hired another pilot, Hank Kohen, to do his flying for him. With his ability to service the North expanded threefold, Ward's business soon took off. He bought a one-room house in Yellowknife and moved Marjorie and their first-born daughter, Gail, to live with him. Ward even scraped together a few thousand dollars to purchase a Bellanca Skyrocket for the company, at the time one of the largest aircraft the North had ever seen. It had three times the capacity of the Moth and could cruise at 110 miles per hour.

But the company's debt was massive, and Ward was becoming increasingly dissatisfied with the partnership. Ward flew every day, sleeping when he could, and sometimes going for days without seeing his family, while Pigeon stayed at home and complained about how the company wasn't making enough money. Pigeon and Ward could also not decide on the best way to run the business. Although Ward and his family could live on the company's meager profits, it was a lot of work for what ultimately turned out to be little financial gain. In the spring of 1949, Ward left Yellowknife Airways. The decision was difficult, but necessary. Ward had always been a player in life, not a spectator, so he didn't enjoy watching someone else run what he felt was his company.

The family moved to Lethbridge, Alberta, that summer where Max found work in construction with Marjorie's father. He was able to make enough money to pay off his debt from buying the Bellanca, but it wasn't long before he felt that familiar itch to be airborne. Within a year, he was hired by Tommy Fox of Associated Airways to do some flying throughout the North. It wasn't the same as running his own business, but better than swinging a hammer. Besides, if Max was ever going to have a run at his own company again, he had to keep flying.

As always, the work was difficult and dangerous. In November 1951, Ward flew a Hudson's Bay Company manager to Bathurst Inlet from Yellowknife. Along the trip, Neil Murphy, Ward's mechanic, asked if they could set down at Muskox Lake to check in on his father, a trapper in the area. Max agreed, but Murphy's father took his time putting in an appearance. By the time he showed up, the sun was beginning to set.

Max knew the instant he took off that they should have camped out for the night. With his compass rendered useless this close to the Magnetic North Pole, Max was flying dead reckoning, navigating from one known point to another by sight and memory. But the sun moved faster than his plane, and it wasn't long before the night sky chased away the blue of day. Fog reached up from the icepack below, obscuring the land to where Max simply couldn't see what was below. With the night sky deepening and the fog worsening, Max decided to set down quickly. He saw what looked like the faint outline of a lake through the ice fog and steered for it.

"If you see something wrong, just holler," he told Murphy.

"If I see it coming—" Murphy replied ominously.

What Max thought was a lake turned out to be the top of a hill, and although Murphy screamed at the top of his lungs to pull up, it was too late. The plane slammed into the top of the hill just behind its skis, bouncing off and back into the air. The engine struggled, the airspeed slowing dramatically, and Max was forced to point the nose down and pray for flat land ahead. Wisps of fog tickled the plane's skin as it came down on the far side of the hill, touching down safely and skidding to a stop.

"How do you not see a hill?" the HBC manager groused from the backseat. Max just shook his head and reached for the radio to call for help.

Help was five days in arriving. His so-called rescuer, a flyer by the name of Abe Dyke, became lost in the Barren Lands, and by the time he had corrected his course, did not have enough fuel to search for Ward and his passenger. An RCAF plane overflew the stranded crew and conveyed their whereabouts to Dyke who was refueling in Bathurst. They made it home safely, but Ward was fired from Associated shortly afterwards when he refused to take a job as manager of the Yellowknife operation.

Ward really didn't mind because he was ready to try his hand at being in business for himself again. Flying was all well and good for some, but Max wanted to run his own airline. With everything he knew about flying in the North and his several business attempts so far, Max felt he could really give larger companies such as Canadian Pacific Airlines (CPA) a run for their money in the bush-flying business. But he needed the right plane to do it.

The right plane, Max decided, was the deHavilland Otter. In the 1950s, deHavilland had decided that the best way to build a bush plane was to ask bush pilots what they wanted in an aircraft. They hired one of the best bush pilots in Canadian history—none other than Clennel Haggerston "Punch" Dickins—to help build the plane. In one of the greatest engineering feats in Canadian history, deHavilland built the Otter, a plane that had a massive payload and was reliable too. It cost a pretty penny, but after begging several banks to help him out, Max was able to scrape enough credit together to make a down payment on the plane. On June 5, 1953, Wardair was born.

Even though the business not an immediate success, Wardair soon developed a towering reputation in the bush as a reliable air service. Business began to flow in. By 1954, Max had added two more planes to his fleet, a deHavilland Beaver and a Fairchild Husky. He purchased an old bunkhouse in Yellowknife and converted it into a hangar, hired two more pilots and an engineer and was actually taking home a salary.

Some of the work Wardair was hired to do proved quite bizarre. On one occasion, an American named John Teel hired Wardair to help capture a musk ox—the horned, woolly-coated animal of the North—and fly it south to the U.S. in order to crossbreed it with cattle. Two planes from Wardair located a herd and flew over it at low altitude to separate the animals. When they broke apart, one plane landed, and several men captured one of the animals, lashed its legs together and placed it in the cargo hold of the plane. Unfortunately for Max, who still helped to clean and service the planes, the animal was not housebroken.

Consolidated Mining also contracted Wardair to fly two gold bars per week out of one of its sites 55 miles north of

Max Ward with his deHavilland Otter, 1953

Yellowknife. The two gold bars represented the mine's weekly output and were to be flown to the company's headquarters in Yellowknife. On one flight, Ward was concentrating more on the flying than on the actions of the miners who were his passengers. One of the miners was actually an accomplished criminal from Australia named Tony Gregson. Gregson had switched the gold bars with lead and hired Max for a lift to High River, where he promptly disappeared. Max didn't discover the lead bars until after he dropped Gregson off. The thief and the gold were never found.

In 1960, Ward defied the opinions of his fellow pilots when he purchased a massive aircraft for his company—a Bristol Freighter. The enormous front-loading aircraft was capable of transporting whole trucks, cars and even other aircraft. It cost Ward a substantial sum, but he was able to capitalize on its payload by carrying large cargo. Wardair was proving successful in the North, but Max soon had his eye on bigger business—passenger service. The problem with operating a passenger service in Canada was that the government did not permit it.

The Canadian government had been late in establishing a coast-to-coast passenger service when it created Trans-Canada Airlines (TCA) in the 1930s. By order of the government, TCA was the only scheduled passenger service with permits to operate in Canada, although CPA, operated by former bush pilot Grant McConachie, was grudgingly permitted to fly the schedules TCA declined. Scheduled service was out of the question for Wardair, but after consulting with several former pilots, Max thought that the next big boom would be in charter air service—flying groups of people where they wanted to go when they wanted to go. Max was determined to make a go of it.

But the government would not allow Max's vision to become reality without a fight. Max's original application to operate his charter service was denied. His application was approved the second time around, but the rules governing charter service in Canada were strict. The company offering the charter could only fly full planeloads of travelers who had all belonged to the same organization for at least six months. No individual sales, no scheduled services and no flights within Canada were permitted. Max accepted the rules with reservation and did his best to follow them. He leased a DC-6 from McConachie at CPA, set up an office on the ground floor of the Hotel Macdonald in Edmonton and got to work.

His first international charter was scheduled in June 1962. Wardair's new DC-6 carried passengers from Edmonton to Copenhagen, Denmark. Max scheduled eight charters in his first year of operation and lost money on all of them to the tune of $350,000. He was forced to return the DC-6 to Grant McConachie and search for a new one, eventually finding a good deal on a used DC-6. But Max saw the DC-6 as just a temporary fix until he could afford to jump into the new era of air transport—the jet age.

Ward knew that the only way his fledgling company could compete with the giants of TCA and CPA was by offering great value. He offered charters at low prices and maintained superior traveler service on all his flights. Steaks became the dinner standard on Wardair, served on fine crockery by smiling, cheerful stewardesses. And after every flight, Max and Marjorie would board the plane and clean it from end to end. As word of Wardair's quality of service got out, his business expanded to London, Manchester, Oslo, Belfast and Amsterdam.

Problems came with the charter service. On one occasion, a group called the Piccadilly Club, supposedly devoted to the study of historic buildings in England, sold memberships to the public, then chartered flights on Wardair using their club's name. Wardair flew a planeload of Piccadilly Club members to London only to learn that the money the travelers had paid to club organizers for their return trip wasn't in the bank. Max swallowed his pride and a huge loss on the trip, flying the entire club home at no cost.

In 1965, Wardair finally purchased its first jet. For $5 million, Max purchased a Boeing 727 passenger jet, a three-engine monstrosity that could carry 120 passengers. Max flew the widow of Cy Becker, a lawyer who had helped Max with his purchases throughout the years, down to Seattle to christen the

jet. Not only did the bottle of champagne not break when Lucy
Becker swung it against the fuselage, it left a dent in Ward's new
$5-million plane!

In 1966, the 727 flew 104 of the 122 charters scheduled for
that year. The jet increased its charter service's range and its
ability to deliver more people to a destination faster than with
the DC-6. To cover the additional cost of operating the jet, Wardair went public in 1967, selling off 350,000 shares. The Canadian Transport Commission, successor to the ATB, also eased
the regulations on charter flights, allowing more than one
group to book a single charter flight. In December of that same
year, the U.S. government gave Wardair permission to fly to
points in the U.S.

Throughout the 1970s, Wardair became a popular choice
for air travel to points abroad. Clubs and groups flocked to
the company's reliable and first-class service. Even the Royal
Family, including Prince Charles and Queen Elizabeth II, flew
Wardair for its tours of northern Canada. The company continued to add routes and planes to its service, purchasing Twin
Otters and Dash 7s for its northern air service. The charter arm
of Wardair added more jets to its service, purchasing two Boeing 707 jets and two 747s by 1975. Ward continued to honor
his bush roots by naming each of his aircraft for famous bush
pilots in Canadian history. The 707s were christened the *Wop
May* and the *Punch Dickins* as a token offering to the men who
contributed to making Ward's vision a reality with their trail-
blazing efforts. Ward himself was rewarded for his vision and
entrepreneurial success in 1973, when he was made a member of the Companion of the Order of Icarus and also awarded
the McKee Trophy for his role in the advancement of aviation
in Canada.

But the 1980s were not kind to Wardair. Just as the company finished construction of a $14 million hangar facility in
Toronto and a $14 million office building, a crippling recession

The *Cy Becker*, the first Boeing jet air charter to fly under the Canadian flag, lands at Edmonton Municipal Airport on April 28, 1966, to a crowd of well-wishers. Ward had taken delivery of the jet earlier in Seattle. Three days later, on May 1, the 727 took off from Vancouver for Greenland on its first intercontinental charter flight carrying members of the V.R. Eaton's Social Club on board.

struck North America. As the Canadian dollar plummeted against the American dollar, Wardair lost money quickly. The company was forced to cut jobs and sell off some its planes to keep cash on hand. The company had already ceased operation of its northern flying service in 1979, but the money saved could not cover enough of its costs. In 1982 alone, the company lost $14 million and Max began to worry.

It wasn't just the recession that was crippling Wardair. Charter regulations continued to punish Max's company. TCA had since evolved into Air Canada and CPA into Canadian Airlines. Both still maintained a monopoly on scheduled service, and regulations still forbade Wardair from applying for any piece of that delicious pie. And by the time the Canadian government relaxed charter regulations in 1984, it was too late for Wardair. Even though the company applied for and got schedules in Canada and abroad, the need to expand its fleet proved to be a heavy burden on the company's bottom line.

Air Canada and Canadian were also too entrenched in the Canadian mentality for clients to consider using Wardair for regularly scheduled service. Travel agents who typically received a commission for selling tickets on Air Canada or Canadian flights had little incentive to promote Wardair. The company was also plagued with problems merging its computer reservation system to the industry's system and had difficulty acquiring good hangar facilities. Passengers flying Wardair at major airports still had to walk out onto the runway to board, while other passengers had the use of enclosed jetways. And even though travelers still raved about the service on Wardair's charter flights, they refused to make Wardair their scheduled service of choice.

In 1988, Max sensed the dream was over. Despite massive discounts on airfares and a generous frequent flyer program, Wardair was projecting a loss of $100 million. Max had been in the business long enough to know when he was in trouble.

He had fought so hard to build his little bush air service into a charter juggernaut, but in the end, the market was simply against him. He was proud of his successes, but he could feel failure looming, and it pained him physically.

On January 18, 1989, Max Ward sold Wardair to a holding company of Canadian Airlines. At $17.25 a share, the total cost of the deal was approximately $250 million. And despite promises to the contrary, Wardair's planes and logos were eventually phased out. Wardair was no more.

What had started as a one-man operation in the dirty, snow-caked streets of Yellowknife had evolved into a multimillion-dollar charter service that spanned the globe. Like Grant McConachie, Max Ward's vision and perseverance were the hallmark traits of every bush pilot who ever roamed the skies. His northern air service, the naming of his planes and tireless groundbreaking whether in the air or in government are proof that, although he became a successful businessman, he always considered himself to be a bush pilot.

CHAPTER NINE

Charles Malcolm "Chuck" McAvoy
1932–1964

AUGUST 2003

It was a beautiful day in Canada's Northwest Territories, that is, as nice as it ever got this close to the Arctic Circle. Temperatures were warm and well above freezing, and in the sky flew wisps of cotton cloud that tangled and mixed in the wind. The few grasses that grew on the edge of the North's infamous Barren Lands swayed gently in the breeze. Nearby, a stand of caribou picked at green shoots that sprang up between the rocks, tossing their heads to keep the insects away from their eyes. It was quiet and peaceful, the northland at its best and most beautiful.

One of the caribou suddenly raised its head in mid-bite and looked up into the sky, alarmed. The rest of the herd froze, each animal slowly casting about before bringing its eyes to the sky. A faint humming was heard to the north, a whirring noise that was out of place in the solitude of the Barren Lands, and the animals began to tremble. Suddenly, over the crest of the hill, a machine exploded into the air above, scattering the caribou. The herd collected itself and darted for safety.

"Look at them run," shouted Curtis Constable, the pilot of the helicopter, to his passengers. They looked out their side windows and marveled at the sight of the graceful animals running in near-perfect synchronicity across the rocky landscape.

The two passengers were geologists, heading out to Lupin Lake just off the border that separated the Northwest Territories from Nunavut. Lester Vanhill, one of the geologists, was surveying the land before him when the helicopter flashed over something strange that didn't grow naturally in the wild. He saw a metal cage with strips of fabric fluttering like flags from its frame.

"Anyone else see that?" he asked into the intercom, but Constable was already turning the helicopter around.

"Yeah, I saw that," Constable muttered. He slowed the chopper as they came about to the location both he and Vanhill had spotted. Below them, a mass of wire and metal tangled with threads of torn cloth came into view. Its outline was unmistakable—the remains of an airplane.

Constable didn't even ask his passengers for permission. He scoured the ground for a landing spot and found one a few hundred yards from the wreckage. Setting the helicopter down carefully, he grabbed his camera and jumped to the ground, his two passengers in tow. He walked briskly and then stopped at the outskirts of the crash.

The rocks around the crash site were littered with fragments of metal, tin cans, clothing and other supplies. Tattered cloth fluttered in the breeze as Constable picked his way through the carnage towards the frame. His stomach hummed with dread as he saw a skull lying on the ground next to plane. They saw other remains still inside the plane, a whole pelvis still buckled into what would have been the pilot's chair, an enormous knife still strapped to the bones of the man long since dead. Other bones sat behind the pilot's seat, piled here and there, having long since yielded their integrity to the elements.

"Hey, look at this!" Vanhill shouted. He'd tiptoed over to the other side of the plane and was now sorting through items on the ground.

Constable made his way over, and Vanhill spread out a ragged piece of fabric in front of him. Stenciled letters jumped out at him, "AVOY."

"Looks like there was more to it, but it was ripped off," said Vanhill, setting the blanket back down.

Constable stooped to pick up what appeared to be a singed wallet that lay half-open on the ground. He gingerly peeled apart the crackling plastic sleeves. The wallet was intact, full of cards. Some were too mangled to read, but one was still in perfect shape—an Alberta Motor Association membership card made out to C.M. McAvoy.

The name rang inside Constable's head like a gong. He had heard the story. Everyone who flew in these parts had heard the story of Chuck McAvoy.

Constable carefully placed the wallet back down on the ground and made his way to the engine of the aircraft. He reached in, found the thin metal plate with the serial number etched into it and pulled. It yielded easily, rusted from almost 40 years of exposure to the northern elements.

"We've got to tell someone about this," Constable shouted excitedly to Vanhill. The three men headed back to the helicopter, where they radioed their find into headquarters and asked that the RCMP be contacted.

After being lost for 39 years, Chuck McAvoy was finally found.

Charles Malcolm McAvoy was born October 5, 1932, in Mirror, Alberta. His father, Jim, worked hard on the railroad to provide a home for his wife, Elsie, and two children, Jim, born in 1930, and Charles. The family only lived in Mirror

Alberta Motor Association membership card, found by helicopter pilot Curtis Constable identifying Chuck McAvoy as the pilot of the wrecked plane

another short year before moving north to Fort Chipewyan, Alberta, where Jim worked in the mining industry. A year later, the family moved to Goldfields in northern Saskatchewan, just south of Uranium City, where they became a family of six when Eva and Goldie were born.

In Goldfields, Charles, or "Chuck" as he'd be known for the rest of his life, was first exposed to flying. Bush planes flew in low over Goldfields, landing on the nearby lake. The docks often had a half dozen planes parked on the water's edge, parts and pieces strewn about the jetty as engineers tinkered with

Fokker Super Universals and Junkers monoplanes. After school, Jim and Chuck walked down to the docks and watched the planes roar in from all directions and set down on the crystal surface of Lake Athabasca, their floats sending up great plumes of water.

The pilots of the planes were a tough, friendly sort who flew endless hours in often-unreliable aircraft, delivering supplies and people to some of Canada's most desolate territory. Certainly in Goldfields the bush plane was a necessity. Neither store nor bakery operated in the town, so the McAvoy family got their food from the land or flown in.

Chuck walked through the ranks of pilots and their engineers, asking questions and demanding rides. He was, even at a young age, flamboyant and cavalier. He didn't like school much, but neither did his big brother Jim. His father was often away working in the mines, and when he did return, he pulled the boys out of school to take them duck and big game hunting. Jim wasn't much of a hunter, but Chuck loved it. He and his father crouched in the deep brush of the northern wilderness, guns in hand, waiting for a lone caribou to appear. That far north, game was plentiful, and Elsie soon became a master chef with all sorts of game, ably cooking whatever her boys brought home.

But as fun as hunting was, both boys were even more captivated by flying. Jim was much more somber than his brother, more levelheaded and reasonable. He was a hard-working young man who also hated school. Chuck was more flighty. He often abandoned any pursuit the instant something more appealing caught his attention. He demanded reward in life, seeking instant gratification from any task rather than letting the task itself be its own reward.

The McAvoys pulled up roots from Goldfields and made their way to Edmonton, Alberta, a town that was reaping the benefits of World War II. Aircraft being leased to the Russians by the Americans to help battle the German invasion of the Soviet Union passed through Edmonton's municipal airport by the thousands, en route to Alaska for the final jump over the Bering Strait. As a result, Edmonton had to develop a modern-day system of air traffic control. But Jim McAvoy, Sr., was not interested in flying. He was interested in mining, and in the 1940s, he started up his own diamond drilling operation in the Northwest Territories. He was away from home more frequently now, working hard on his business, starting several small companies to service the vast mineral riches of the North. His camps were numerous but isolated. No roads had been built in the North, or trails. The most efficient way to travel was by air, but there were not enough pilots and planes to support the demand. So Jim, Sr., decided to cut out the middleman, and he bought a plane of his own, a Fox Moth. The plane made trips between camps and even stopped in Edmonton from time to time for supplies. Jim and Chuck often rode in the plane, even handled the controls occasionally. Although they weren't supposed to, the boys learned the basics of flying under the tutelage of their father's employees.

On one occasion, Chuck was on his way north to visit his father. The plane rides were the best part of Chuck's life. He wanted to fly. He didn't want to learn how; he just wanted to be able to do it. The pilot gave Chuck the stick for a little while, but then promptly took it away when Chuck bounced the plane all over the sky. Sullen, Chuck sulked in his seat, arms crossed in fury.

Then, the engine quit.

Chuck unwrapped his arms and stared at the pilot, who was busy working the throttles, trying to restart the engine. Unable to do so, he pushed forward on the collective, putting the plane into a steep dive in an attempt to gain speed so that he could keep the plane aloft. Chuck reached for his seat belt and ratcheted it tightly. He peered out the window straight ahead, into the bush below and saw the trees coming up quickly. But the pilot was good. By diving, he'd been able to generate enough airspeed to maintain a steady glide and had lined himself up with a river that looked wide enough to land the plane.

"Hang on, Chuck," he told the boy. "If I let anything happen to you, your daddy would have my head!"

The plane gently descended until the floats kissed the surface of the water. Chuck sat in his chair rigidly, his hands gripping the sides, waiting for his untimely demise. Instead, the plane landed almost perfectly on the river and skipped along the water's surface before coming to a stop just offshore.

Chuck's pilot got out of the plane quickly. Chuck followed, climbing out of the Fox Moth onto the ground. The pilot began handing him things from the cargo area—an ax, a fire-starter and a kettle—telling him to go and light a fire. As Chuck wormed his way through the tree line, chopping at kindling for a fire, the terror he had felt on landing was replaced with a sense of adventure. Here he was, stranded in the bush, with only his wits to survive. To the teenage boy, the romantic idea only reinforced his already heady ideas about flying. Maybe they'd have to stay here for days, hunt their own food and set up some kind of shelter. Maybe they'd have to float the plane down the river to the next settlement or hike five days to get help. Chuck became increasingly excited, buzzing from tree to tree. He hummed as he chopped wood, and then he bounded back to the plane and built a fire.

Within minutes a crackling blaze was roaring away, and Chuck warmed himself. The pilot, looking tired and frustrated, came over and dumped a handful of leaves onto the fire. The once-pleasant blaze became a sooty beacon of smoke that stretched up into the sky. Within hours, Chuck's bush adventure came to an end when a Seabee, flown by Charlie Fox, roared over the horizon and settled onto the river. Chuck was bundled into the plane and whisked away to a nearby base, where his father was waiting. As the plane pulled up off the river, Chuck shuddered with pleasure.

"I'm going to be a pilot," he told Fox.

"Well, you've certainly had a good start, haven't you?" Fox replied. Chuck was too young to know the man was joking.

Chuck and his mom eventually moved to the Northwest Territories during the war, reuniting their family that had been split between Edmonton and Yellowknife. Two years earlier, Jim, Jr., had been suspended from the Edmonton school system for punching out a school principal who had taken it upon himself to try to teach Jim a harsher lesson than school normally offered. Since no other school in Edmonton would take him after the incident, Jim moved to Yellowknife to live with his father and re-enroll in school. By the time Chuck and his mother arrived in Yellowknife, Jim already had his pilot's license and was flying for his father. Chuck was also learning to fly, using every opportunity to pester his father's other pilots with questions and demonstrations. Some of the men were helpful, some were grouchy, but almost all of them agreed that the young McAvoy boy, although eager, was not very skilled. No sooner would they pass the controls over to him than they were forced to take them back, as the boy would put the plane into some kind of trouble.

When Chuck finished school, he worked for his father's diamond mine drilling operation supervising some of the workers. His dream to fly was put on hold for another pursuit—money. To learn to fly he needed cash, so he took whatever work his father offered him and tried to bank the cash. But it was hard. Chuck was a spender, known for lavishing drinks and good times on his friends. He loved to enjoy himself, and his paychecks were often too far apart for his liking. He gambled on cards and bought cigarettes by the carton as he tried the best he could to shroud the life of a northern worker with good times and laughter.

On one occasion, Jim and Chuck were headed home late one night from a beer parlor, when an RCMP officer pulled over their car. Smelling alcohol, the officer invited Jim back to his vehicle to have a chat about what they'd been up to. As the officer listened, he flipped through a list of outstanding charges and came across the name Jim McAvoy...several times.

"Says here you've been a busy boy, Mr. McAvoy," the officer commented as he read the list.

Jim was floored. Looking over the list, it showed that he had three outstanding charges, mostly traffic offenses. But he figured out what had happened. When he got back to the car, a fistful of tickets in hand, he promptly shoved them all at Chuck.

"Is this you?" he asked his brother.

Chuck swallowed, then began to laugh. Jim couldn't help himself and laughed as well.

By the age of 25, Chuck had obtained his pilot's license and flew for his dad's diamond drilling company for a few years. The company bought a Stinson Reliant, and Chuck and Jim were flying almost full time for their dad. Whatever was needed that could be put aboard a plane, the boys flew it. Dynamite, food, whole diamond drills...the loads often made the plane noticeably heavier so that it sometimes took a little extra effort to get the plane into the air.

Chuck obtained his operator's license, but he still didn't have a commercial pilot's license, which was necessary for him to be gainfully employed as a pilot. He didn't share that information with his clients or with his father and brother.

But he didn't need to hide that he was now married. His bride's name was Gwen Ralston, a divorcée who had once been married to a mechanic at a rival air service. The divorce had been quick; it was rumored that Gwen had been found in a compromising position in the backseat of a car on the outskirts of town with a man who was not her husband. But the stories didn't bother Chuck. He loved Gwen and doted on her. When the two married, Chuck beamed. Jim was quiet in his support of the union, the rumors of Gwen's behavior too fresh in his mind. He didn't much care for her, but kept it to himself.

Meanwhile, Chuck was regularly getting himself into trouble in the air. His enthusiasm and grandiosity often eclipsed his skill and judgment, and it was by the grace of God he survived. Taking a group of miners north on one occasion, Chuck put the plane down on a lake that was simply too small. The plane ran up on the shore and some feet into the bush before coming to a halt. Although the miners were happy with their location, Chuck was not. He barely had enough room to land the plane and now did not have nearly enough room to take off. When he radioed in to base, it fell to his brother Jim to rescue him. As the Fairchild carrying Jim and Chuck barely cleared the tree line of the lake, Jim pointed wordlessly out the window. Only a few hundred yards to the east was a lake easily three times the size of the one Chuck had landed on.

Months later, Chuck flew to Fort Smith with a load of supplies for a mining camp. He got away late, the sun already setting as he took off, but he decided to push it anyway. He'd been lazy not to leave earlier, but the men at the mining camp needed the shipment. Flying at night was not permitted by the Department of Transportation, but Chuck didn't care much for the rules. He'd been warned about flying too late at night or too late in the season, but paid little attention.

It became completely dark once the sun had set, and Chuck couldn't see where he was going. An hour out, he thought to look at his fuel gauge and realized with a start that the needle was on empty. He looked around desperately but could see nothing—no treetops, water or open ground, just empty, inky darkness all around. He had no idea where he could land. Moments later, the engine sputtered, then stopped altogether. He would just have to put down right where he was. Keeping an eye on the altimeter, Chuck flipped on his lights and realized with horror that he was coming down in the middle of a farmer's field. The problem was that he didn't have wheels on the plane; he had floats.

The floats managed to hold the plane up but were destroyed in the rough landing. Again, Jim was forced to rescue his brother and help him complete the job. Again, he said nothing to Chuck about his behavior.

Chuck also wasn't as gifted as other pilots when it came to mechanical know-how. Some pilots could repair their engines in the middle of the bush with nothing but a set of tools, a stick of gum and an old water pipe. Others made modifications to their planes to gain greater horsepower, increased range or more efficient flight. On one noteworthy occasion, Chuck decided fill the floats of the Stinson with Styrofoam, thinking that the foam would add buoyancy to the floats and allow the plane to ride higher out of the water on takeoff and landing. Chuck was surprised when he returned an hour later to find the plane had sunk down past its floats and was now resting on the floor of the lake. Rather than help lift the floats, the Styrofoam had sucked up water like a sponge, making the floats heavier and pulling them under. Again, Jim arrived to help pull the plane to shore, and the two dug the sopping foam out of the floats. Again, Jim said nothing.

Chuck was also gullible. A chef at one of the more isolated camps was looking for a free ride back to civilization. He telegraphed Chuck to say that he was having one of the worst toothaches of his life and was in urgent need of a dentist. Chuck flew to the camp and back to Yellowknife, the cook moaning and holding his jaw the entire way. When Chuck told the story to his co-workers later that night, he was surprised when everyone started to laugh at him. It turned out that the cook had lost the last of his teeth many years before.

In 1960, the brothers started their own air service out of Yellowknife. Deciding that McAvoy Air Service needed better planes, Chuck caught a train to Winnipeg where he negotiated a deal on a used plane. When asked to produce his commercial pilot's license, Chuck was unable to do so because he still did not have one. No license, no plane. Chuck telegraphed his brother, who arrived some days later in a foul mood, and he flew the two of them home.

The North was open to excavation in the 1960s as Canada's mining companies penetrated farther and farther into the barrens in search of minerals and precious metals. Diamonds were big business in the North, but so were uranium and gold. But the government had not seen fit to build any roads. The tundra simply couldn't handle the sustained beating of heavy road traffic. The best way to travel was still by plane, and the McAvoy brothers profited from the situation. While Jim took care of the paperwork, Chuck, who had finally obtained his commercial pilot's license, focused solely on flying. They moved construction materials all across the North, as well as mining equipment and men.

Despite his enthusiasm, Chuck was still often careless in his work. In April 1960, against the advice of other pilots who knew the ice was too thin, Chuck took a load of supplies to a camp north of Yellowknife. The landing at the camp was fine, but on the return trip, Chuck put the plane through a sheet of ice too thin to support its weight. As a result, Jim and Chuck were forced to wait several weeks until the ice had completely melted before they could get the plane out. Months later, Chuck flew the superintendent of the Department of Transport across the North, showing off his air service to the man. As the two flew over the lake, Chuck put the plane into a gentle dive to get a closer look at a group of fishing boats collected on Great Slave Lake. So focused was he on the boats that he didn't notice his altimeter spiraling downwards. When he did finally pull up, he was rewarded with the smack of something hitting the bottom of the plane. The plane wobbled in the air then steadied itself. Chuck looked back to see a fisherman standing on the deck of his boat and shaking his fist at the plane that had just taken off the top of his mast.

When Chuck wasn't flying, he and Gwen were traveling. With the money the company made, Chuck left the business in his brother's hands and set off for exciting destinations with Gwen—Toronto, New York and Las Vegas. And while there, Chuck bent any ear he could find, regaling those around him with tales of mercy flights, finding lost pilots and being stranded with only survival skills and a small tin of rations.

"If I ever get lost," he boasted, "no one will ever find me."

Money was coming in from the business, but Chuck took the bulk of it to satisfy his wife and family. Gwen hated the North, but came to life on their trips as the two found new friends, attended parties and gambled in the casinos of Las Vegas.

Back in the North, Chuck seldom participated in any real mercy flights or search-and-rescue missions. But on one occasion, he and his brother were taking a load of supplies across the Nahanni when Chuck suddenly steered south, saying that he just wanted to check something. The letters "S.O.S." soon flashed up from the ground at them, stamped in the snow. Chuck put the plane down immediately. What they found was horrifying. A prospecting party had been dropped off several months earlier and forgotten. Only two of what had been a party of five remained barely alive. With limited food and ammunition, it was only a matter of time before they were all starving. Two prospectors had set out on foot, looking for help and were never seen again. A third, in agony over his starvation, strapped a belt of dynamite to his chest and walked out into the woods. The two survivors heard a bang, and the man never came back.

The brothers flew the two survivors back to Yellowknife for medical treatment. Jim never figured out how Chuck knew to fly in the direction of the camp. It had been out of their way, yet Chuck had insisted. Jim never asked, and his intuition told him he was probably better off not knowing.

At home in Yellowknife, Jim kept up the same hectic pace, cultivating clientele and taking care of all the paperwork. He felt the tension taking hold, clawing at his chest. Time after time, Chuck came to him with another story of some mishap that was supposed to make Jim laugh. But Jim wasn't laughing anymore. He was overworked. He never got to go traveling or partying. He stayed home and minded the fort while Chuck fed his wife's ego. Jim was tired of it.

One summer, Chuck overturned an ex-police boat in the middle of a particularly violent storm while trying to deliver a diamond drill to a destination across Great Slave Lake. He lost both the boat and the drill. Jim finally snapped. He was tired of his brother's antics, tired of the work, tired of the company's money being gobbled up. When his brother returned from the ill-fated boat incident, Jim let him have it. Having kept quiet for so many years, having pulled his brother out of so many precarious situations, Jim decided to leave his brother. Chuck was flabbergasted, but Jim was firm.

"You're going to be dead by the time you're 33," Jim growled, as he walked out the office door for the last time.

The two never spoke after that.

Chuck worked hard over the next few years to keep the business operating, but it was tough work. Taking care of all the menial tasks as well as the flying proved beyond his capabilities. He began to let things go—missing contracts and skipping regular maintenance work. He flew longer and longer hours, working during April and November when the ice was beginning to melt or was just beginning to form, a time when most pilots parked their planes and waited until the lakes were clear or frozen over. He flew at night, much later than regulations allowed, in a plane that was often barely flightworthy. He still found the time and money to keep Gwen happy, taking her on trips. The Pink Flamingo Casino in Las Vegas even issued him a V.I.P. card because he was there so often.

But the work was lonely without Jim. Chuck missed his brother terribly, but neither he nor Jim could ever bring themselves to speak to one another. Chuck's allegiance was to his wife and two children, but he often wished it otherwise.

In June 1964, a pair of curious figures contacted Chuck. The two were American mining graduates from the University of Minnesota. Albert Kunes, 24, and Doug Torp, 23, had made their way north in search of gold. They worked for Roberts Mining out of Duluth and were eager to get into the field. They got in touch with Chuck in Bristol Lake, seeking transportation to a camp at Itchen Lake in the Northwest Territories. Chuck agreed to their terms and told them to be ready to take off on June 9.

The night before the trip, Chuck took the time to give his 1932 Fairchild 82 a once-over. It was in rough shape, dirty and banged up, the wood fuselage warped in places, and stress marks showing on the undercarriage. But after a quick look, Chuck decided it would fly just fine. He looked down at the skis on his plane and wondered for the dozenth time since April if it wasn't time to get the floats on, or at least some wheels. He stood back from the plane and considered it, then tiredly wiped his hand across his face and headed inside for bed.

On the morning of June 9, a freak storm rolled in to the Northwest Territories and roared through the tiny settlement of Bristol Lake, sharp pellets of snow lashing the ground. Both Kunes and Torp were certain the trip would be put off another day and were unpacking their gear when the door to their cabin flew open and McAvoy burst through the door.

Chuck McAvoy's 1938 Fairchild 82A, July 1962

"Don't let a little bit of snow, scare you boys!" he roared. "You're in the hands of one of the best pilots in the North!"

But the weather was worse than Chuck let on. He'd already spoken with one of the pilots from Wardair who had tried to take off earlier that morning but abandoned the attempt. Wardair had canceled flights for the whole day until the weather cleared, but Chuck couldn't afford that luxury. He had other jobs in the next few days. Pushing back this job could mean losing work elsewhere, and he wasn't about to take that risk.

He felt sick to his stomach as he climbed into the Fairchild and showed his two young passengers where to stow their belongings. As he sailed through his preflight checklist, his stomach became more and more queasy. He wondered if Wardair might not have the right idea. He looked outside into the snow and could barely see 10 feet in front of the plane. His stomach flip-flopped again. But time was money, and Chuck didn't have much extra time to spare. He'd flown in worse, he was sure, and would come through this one just fine.

The wind buffeted the Fairchild as Chuck brought the plane around, rocking it from side to side, its wail amplified inside the plane. Chuck opened the throttles to full power and sent the plane into the sky, his hands tight on the stick as he fought to keep the plane steady. As the Fairchild gained more and more speed, he climbed higher and higher, fighting through the clouds to bring the plane on course for Itchen Lake.

The flight was long and harrowing for the intrepid threesome as the Fairchild clawed its way through the storm. Chuck smoked cigarettes to calm his nerves and tried to joke with his passengers, but Kunes and Torp were having none of it. The two had flown before, but never in weather this bad and never in such a rickety old plane. They sat glued to their seats, staring straight ahead, trying to see through the storm. Chuck laughed nervously at his own jokes, talking nonstop as his stomach rose and fell with every dip. The nausea he'd felt on takeoff had not diminished; it had gotten worse. Chuck knew deep down that flying in this weather had been a terrible idea.

"Nothing I can do about it now," he thought out loud.

"What?" Kunes asked him sharply, eyes worried.

"Just something with the missus," Chuck covered quickly, lighting up a fresh cigarette. "You know how dames can be. Why, one time I was—"

He heard it. Kunes and Torp didn't, but Chuck did—a gentle bang, a hiccup muffled in the roar of the storm. The plane lurched gently, imperceptibly to the inexperienced. His body hummed with adrenaline, and the roof of his mouth felt as if it had been stabbed. Chuck checked his gauges but could see nothing wrong.

A second bang sounded, this one definitely from the engine. And this time, his passengers heard it.

"What was that?" Kunes demanded, gripping the side of his chair in fear.

"I honestly don't know," Chuck responded, frowning. "Probably just something minor. We should be okay."

Another bang echoed through the cabin, and Torp started in fear. The roar of the Fairchild's engine dipped substantially then roared to life again. The plane seemed to stop in midair, then slowly speed up again.

Chuck checked his instruments and looked down at his map. They were on course, 100 miles south of Bathurst Inlet. According to the map, Lupin Lake should be just below them. Chuck chewed his lip and made his decision.

"I'm going to put her down so I can check the engine out," he yelled as the engine backfired again. "Just hang on tight. Don't worry so much. I've done this 100 times!"

Chuck checked his instruments again and pushed forward gently on the stick, nosing the plane towards the ground. As the altimeter spun down slowly, Chuck stared straight ahead, searching for the outline of Lupin Lake. At 500 feet, he saw it, dead ahead, still iced over and covered in snow from the storm. Chuck's shoulders hurt from holding on to the controls so tightly, and he felt the beginnings of a headache. But he put both those things out of his mind as he concentrated on lining the plane up with the smooth, white blanket of snow ahead. He breathed a sigh of relief, confident he was on course.

"See? Nothing to worry about!" he shouted to his passengers, who both exhaled noticeably. Chuck reached over and punched Kunes in the shoulder playfully, then brought his head around to check his final approach. He stopped. His eyes went wide, and he froze in his chair.

He had misjudged the distance to the lake. Instead of smooth ice and pristine white powder, the jagged tips of boulders and rocks were coming up fast.

He did not react. He had no time to pull up, no time to hit the throttle, no time to warn his passengers, no time to throw his head between his knees for protection. As the skis of the Fairchild slammed down on the rock bed surrounding the lake, Chuck only had time for one thought.

Jim won't be coming to get me this time.

The Fairchild smacked into the ground at high speed; the skis ripped off, the plane spun out of control. The fuselage tore open, exposing aviation fuel to the sparks generated from the crash. One spark caught the fuel and followed the trail of gas back to the tanks, which were still half full. The Fairchild exploded, scattering flaming debris everywhere.

But Chuck McAvoy was already dead.

When word reached Yellowknife that Chuck McAvoy had not arrived at Itchen Lake as planned, the response was overwhelming. Nearly a dozen pilots took to the air, some flying as many as 50 hours in a week, looking for any sign of Chuck or his plane. The Royal Canadian Air Force launched a rescue mission to look for the plane. The U.S. government, concerned for the well-being of Kunes and Torp, sent two planes and a squad of soldiers to scour the NWT's dreaded Barren Lands for any sign of a crash. After two weeks of endless flying and hiking, the search was called off. In two solid weeks, no one had found any sign of the wreckage.

In Edmonton, Elsie McAvoy held out hope. For months after the crash, she waited for her son to come walking out of the woodlands, full of stories of living off the land and having to hike out of the wilderness back to civilization. Maybe he'd

The remains of Chuck McAvoy's plane were found on the boundary of the NWT Barren Lands in August 2003.

been taken in by some nice Inuit family, she thought, or he had built himself a cabin in the wild. Sometimes pilots crashed and were missing for days, even weeks at a time and they were written off as dead, and days later, they'd hike out of the forest. But most did not.

Chuck McAvoy's remains and those of his passengers were found on August 9, 2003.

❧◆❧

FEBRUARY 9, 2004

He starts to talk slowly, haltingly, his voice higher than
I expected, his words a little slurred with age. But I'm not
fooled by appearances. As Jim McAvoy talks, I detect the sharp
mind that still lives beneath the aging exterior. He quit flying
only five years earlier, when he could no longer pass the flight
medical exam. He tells me he'd still be flying if they let him.

The house in Thorsby, Alberta, is home to many dogs, most
of them mixed breeds that I can't identify. There are at least
four or five, some outside, some inside. A small, curly haired
dog with gray, almost purple, fur sits beside Jim as the two of
us sit and talk about his history and his brother.

Jim and I sit in his living room, drinking coffee and eating
lemon tarts. He shows me pictures of his flying days, of northern communities from the sky and of all the planes he's flown.
The more he talks, the more he has to say. He begins to regale
me with stories of night flying, of landing in a lumberyard, of
having his license suspended lord knows how many times.
And slowly he begins to talk a little about his brother.

As he talks, he reaches out for the purple-haired dog, petting
it along its back with long, smooth strokes. The more he talks
about Chuck, the harder he pets the dog. With every story, the
poor pooch looks like it's one stroke away from a broken bone.

Jim doesn't think Chuck was a very good pilot. He can't
think, despite the reports in the media since the wreckage of
Chuck's plane was found, of a single instance in which Chuck
ever found a lost pilot. He was irresponsible and lacked sound
judgment.

He bows his head to the dog at his feet, clutching its head
tightly, grabbing its fur and stretching it back as he drops his
head and shoulders.

"Wasn't a very good pilot. One simple way to tell." He looks up, not at me, but over my head at the wall behind me, avoiding eye contact.

"He's not here today."

And with that, he lets the dog go.

CHAPTER TEN

The MacAlpine Expedition and Search

August 24–December 4, 1929

EXPEDITION
OCTOBER 21, 1929

The feeling of being suffocated woke him. He didn't hear the crack of the ice, didn't hear the shifting of the ice blocks. He was sound asleep, too tired to hear such small sounds. Wrapped in his sleeping bag, exhausted and malnourished, George "Tommy" Thompson was used to the mournful wail of the north wind, used to the frigid temperatures, and he was even used to the loud, ripping snores of his bunkmates. After a month stranded in the Barren Lands of the North, Tommy could sleep through almost anything.

Suddenly, he couldn't breathe, and he awoke with a start. He felt something on him, felt icy cold on his face. He panicked, wondering if he was drowning. Maybe he had fallen through the ice in his sleep, and he was sinking into the bone-numbing waters of the Arctic Ocean.

He shook his head from side to side and writhed in his sleeping bag, trying to get free. He exhaled forcefully and felt something give. Reflexively, he gasped, inhaling deeply. His thrashing, the rustle of fabric and the crunch of snow were lost in the roar of arctic wind as he struggled to free himself. Something was on top of him, holding him down.

Then hands were on him, calming hands, and he heard a gentle shush over the sounds of his struggle. He stopped his frantic squirming and listened.

"Easy, Tommy. Easy!" A voice came next to his ear. "Just relax, and we'll get you out."

A finger stabbed at his eye, wiping flecks of snow away. Tommy blinked frantically to clear the rest, but he could see only darkness. He craned his neck, looked down at his feet and saw several large blocks of snow on top of him. Shadows hustled around him, grabbing the blocks and tossing them off to the side.

Tommy laid back and tried to relax. He stared up and found himself looking into the night sky. Countless stars flickered above, and Tommy thought that was strange because he thought they'd built an igloo last night.

Finally, the last of the snow blocks was cleared, and many more hands grabbed at him, pulling him out of his sleeping bag and onto his feet. Tommy dusted himself off and brushed the rest of the snow away from his face. Looking down, he saw tumbled cubes of snow littering the ground around him and seven other men also shaking snow from their clothes.

"What happened?" Tommy shouted over the wind.

"The igloo collapsed," Colonel C.D. MacAlpine, leader of the expedition, shouted back. "We've got to get it put back together! We need our rest if we're going to make it the rest of the way!"

Another man clapped Tommy's shoulder. "You all right?" Major Robert Baker asked.

"Fine, fine," Tommy replied. "What time is it?"

The Colonel shrugged, "Near as I can tell, it's about three in the morning. Bloody cold, too."

Baker looked around him as the rest of the party gathered, all of them clutching themselves to try and hold in what little heat their bodies could still generate. Even in the dark, Tommy could see their drooping eyes, bony cheeks and pale, cracked skin. These men were sickly, tired, cold and starving. They'd spent almost two months in the bush and were now stranded on the frozen icepack of the Arctic Ocean with nothing around for miles but darkness and ice. But they were standing now and ready to work.

Tommy looked over at the other two igloos in camp. Not so much as a head poked out of the small ice huts. Their Inuit guides either hadn't heard their igloo implode or had heard, but didn't care.

Tommy bent down and began sorting through the scattered blocks of ice, throwing away the broken ones. Morning was hours away and Cambridge Bay days still. If they were going to make it back to civilization, they needed rest.

But, Tommy thought to himself, with their luck so far, that was a pretty big *if*.

❧❖❧

EXPEDITION
AUGUST 27, 1929

"Tommy…Tommy…Tommy…! Wake up, buddy!"

Half conscious, Tommy batted at the voice that pulled him from sleep and mumbled something incoherent. A finger poked at his chest, and Tommy roared even more incoherently, chopping at the offending digit.

"Dammit, Tommy!" a stern voice cursed. "Get the hell out of bed! We've got a problem!"

Tommy opened his eyes and came face to face with his boss at Dominion Explorers, Colonel C.D. MacAlpine, aka "the

Colonel." Mostly a pleasant, energetic man, today his face was scrunched in a heavy scowl, and his eyes radiated sheer rage.

"What is it, sir?" Tommy managed, sitting up on one elbow and jabbing a knuckle into his sleep-encrusted eyes.

"SP is gone, that's what!" the Colonel roared.

"What do you mean, gone, sir?" Tommy replied, confused.

"I mean the ruddy plane is gone, Tommy!" the Colonel shouted. "Get dressed. We need to go look for it."

Tommy swung out of his bunk, dressed and followed the Colonel out to the kitchen. It was still early, not quite 8:00 AM, and the clouds outside did not look promising. Getting here had been problem enough, Tommy remembered. Now, to have one of their planes just gone...

The rest of the expedition was gathered in the kitchen of the Hudson's Bay Company outpost at Fort Churchill, sipping coffee and wolfing down breakfast. All wore the same look of concern on their faces. Not three days into their journey, they were already behind schedule.

It was to be the most ambitious undertaking in the history of commercial air travel. Fresh off his pioneering flight across the Barren Lands with flying legend Punch Dickins, the Colonel returned home convinced of the utility of the airplane. He bought his own planes, hired pilots for his company and began flying men and machinery across the North. His men were soon infiltrating previously uncharted, unexplored territories and uncovering major strikes of minerals. The investment in the flying machines paid off handsomely, and now MacAlpine wanted his own name in the record books.

It would be the longest round-trip by plane ever. Colonel MacAlpine, along with seven other crew members divided between two of the Dominion Explorer planes, a Fokker Super Universal, G-CASP (SP), and a Fairchild, CF-AAO (AO), took off from Winnipeg on August 24. The plan was to check in on as many mining sites as possible along a route that, once completed, would total more than 22,000 miles. From Winnipeg, the two planes would hop to Baker Lake in the Northwest Territories, to Bathurst Inlet, Fort Norman and Aklavik on the tip of the Yukon before returning home. Along the way, they would drop off supplies, do some exploring and pick up a few prospectors who were due for a trip home.

Had the Colonel believed in something more otherworldly than his planes and men, he might have thought that the events of the first three days of the trip were ominous and called it off. Almost immediately upon leaving Winnipeg, the planes flew headlong into thick, billowing smoke from a raging forest fire. They were forced down twice, using up precious fuel as they buzzed through the smokescreen far below cruising speed. With the needle on his fuel gauge creeping ever lower, Tommy, who was flying the Colonel, Richard Pearce, editor of the newspaper *Northern Miner,* and air engineer Dan Goodwin, decided to put down at nearby Jackfish Isles to top up his tanks. Tommy was chagrined, however, to find the fuel cache at Jackfish empty, sucked dry by some other pilot. Tommy took the plane back into the air, and defying the smoke from the forest fire, made it to Fort Churchill on nothing but fumes.

To make matters worse, when the two planes arrived at Fort Churchill on August 26, they discovered that their supply ship, the schooner *Morso,* had not. The schooner carried spare fuel, tools and food the explorers needed to complete their flight safely. Without it, the mission could not continue.

Later that day, the men of the expedition heard a voice cry out, and they all ran down to the waterfront. Two rowboats crept up to the shoreline and disgorged a score of sweaty, soot-covered sailors. The *Morso,* the sailors explained, had caught fire, and the crew was forced to abandon ship. As soon as the sailors had made their way to their lifeboats and paddled away a safe distance, the fire reached the dynamite stored in the *Morso*'s hold. The ship and MacAlpine's supplies were gone.

Undaunted, the Colonel purchased the supplies the expedition would need from the HBC outpost at Fort Churchill and informed his crew that they were leaving in the morning. Both of the expedition's planes were anchored down before nightfall, chained to the bottom of the Hudson Bay by a length of metal and a 500-pound anchor.

But that, it seemed, was not enough to hold SP in place. AO was still where she had been anchored, but SP was gone, and no one could see her, even with field glasses.

The crew was just preparing to search for SP from the air using AO when another ship appeared on the horizon. The S.S. *Arcadia* and her crew had found SP.

The plane, it seemed, had drifted well out to sea before taking on water and sinking. But one wing still poked out of the glassy surface of the bay. The crew of the *Arcadia* had noticed her and attached a line, trying to lift SP aboard ship. But the line couldn't handle the machine, and when the line snapped, the plane sank right to the bottom. When the *Arcadia* pulled up her anchor to continue on to Fort Churchill, SP came up, hooked to the anchor. But the plane was no longer in flying condition, so the Colonel sent word to Winnipeg to send another plane to Fort Churchill so that the expedition could continue. While waiting for the replacement plane, the crew almost lost AO as well when the Fairchild also drifted out to sea overnight. But the tug *Graham Bell* recovered her and pulled her back to shore and to her anxious pilot, Stan McMillan.

On September 6, World War I flying ace Roy Brown, who was credited with shooting down the infamous Red Baron in the skies over Europe, arrived in Fort Churchill with another Fokker Super Universal, G-CASK. SK had already seen her share of action, flying MacAlpine, Pearce and Punch Dickins across the Barren Lands one year earlier. She was ready to conquer the North yet again, and the Colonel gave orders that the expedition would leave early the next day.

At 10:00 AM, SK and AO took to the skies, much to the relief of the Colonel and the crews. By the end of the day, they had reached Baker Lake, 200 miles west of Chesterfield Inlet. Picking up a load of fuel and an eighth passenger—Major Robert Baker—the crew set off the next morning, easily reaching the next stage of their journey, Beverley Lake. As the pilots and engineers fueled the planes for their next hop to Bathurst Inlet, the Colonel and Pearce stood at the water's edge, the Colonel smoking and Pearce frantically taking notes.

"What's a little bad luck?" said the Colonel to the diminutive newspaper reporter. "I figure, bad luck comes in threes," he began to tick off on his fingers. "Ship blowing up, SP blowing away, AO blowing away. I figure we're through that now, and it's smooth sailing from here on."

"Can I quote you on that?" Pearce asked.

"Absolutely, my boy," MacAlpine replied confidently.

With both planes being so close to the Magnetic North Pole, their compasses were unreliable, swinging wildly in circles. Instead, the crews were using old-style sun compasses to plot their direction. But because sun compasses were not the most reliable navigation instruments, the crew planned to fly as far north as possible, then along the coast of the Arctic Ocean until they arrived at Bathurst Inlet. A large body of water was located south of Bathurst where Tommy and Stan would land and refuel their planes. When morning came, both aircraft soared into the sky once more, passing Perry Lake just before noon and continuing west. On sighting a large lake off in the distance, McMillan waggled his wings to get Tommy's attention and began to descend. When the planes landed, the pilots realized that they had no earthly idea where they were. The lake on which they had landed did not correspond to any lake on their maps. Frustrated, both pilots took off again and began searching for the route to Bathurst.

As soon as they took off, the weather turned foul. Rain, snow, wind and bitter cold socked in both planes. The flying machines bucked against gale-force winds, and because the sun was hidden behind the clouds, neither pilot had a clue as to the correct route. To make matters worse, both SK and AO were dangerously low on fuel.

As the planes swooped in below the clouds to have a closer look at the land below, Dan Goodwin, the engineer aboard SK, called out to Tommy when he saw a small Inuit camp on the shore of the lake.

"They might know where the blazes we are," Goodwin reasoned. Tommy agreed and set the plane down on the lake.

Disembarking from the plane, the eight men of the MacAlpine expedition slogged their way to shore to ask for directions. A young Inuit man stepped out of his camp to greet the men who had arrived in the flying machines.

The Native, whom the expedition members decided to nickname "Joe," spoke no English, nor did his wife or the other man in the small camp. Sitting down on the dirt, Tommy grabbed a stick and drew a crude map on the ground and, pointing with his fingers, he managed to communicate his intentions to Joe. Joe grabbed the stick from Tommy and marked an X on a point just north of where they were.

Tommy pointed at the plane, then at Joe, asking if Joe would be kind enough to show them the way. Joe smiled, showing rotten teeth and nodded enthusiastically.

"Who says we're so different?" Tommy asked his mates, smiling.

The weather, however, kept them grounded for another three days. The men camped out in their sleeping bags in the grasses and weeds just off the shores of the lake. MacAlpine ordered an inventory of their supplies, and the engineers and pilots worked on the planes, transferring the fuel left in AO over to SK for the trip to Bathurst Inlet.

On takeoff, SK's engine struggled, and the engineers discovered that ice had formed inside the plane's carburetor. Pulling the two planes side by side, the crew transferred all the fuel they could from SK back into AO. Tommy Thompson, along with the Colonel, Dan Goodwin and their new friend Joe took off just after noon on September 12 bound for Bathurst Inlet for fuel and supplies. The sky was heavy with fog when the plane disappeared into the distance. The men left behind settled in for a long wait, smoking and breaking out a deck of cards in their tent.

Twenty minutes later, the buzz of an airplane reached their ears, and they all turned to watch AO alight upon the surface of the lake once again. When the plane reached the shore, Tommy and the Colonel hopped out, shaking their heads. Joe dismounted awkwardly, his limbs stiff with fear.

"Can't see a bloody thing up there," Tommy told the rest of the party. "And there's next to no gas in the plane. Don't think we'd make it to Bathurst anyway. No sense in getting lost in two different places." The men were silent. They were miles from help, and no one knew where they were. The Colonel cleared his throat and spoke.

"All right, men, this is no time to feel sorry for ourselves," he said. "It's going to be difficult, but we can handle it. I left instructions for the crew back in Winnipeg to start searching if they hadn't heard from us in 10 days, so I don't think we'll be here for long."

He began to pace back and forth in front of the men, voicing his thoughts as they struck him, thinking out loud.

"That's not to say we shouldn't plan for it. We need discipline now, more than anything. As of right now, all food will be rationed as sparingly as possible. Major Baker will be in

The camp of the members of the ill-fated MacAlpine expedition at Dease Point in the fall of 1929. Lost in the Northwest Territories without enough gasoline to fly back to civilization, the members of the expedition were forced to live off the land and the good graces of their Inuit neighbors before hiking back to civilization. The crew camped in the tent (left) while they constructed the five-foot high sod hut in which all of them would live (right). Engineers with the party originally tried to use a wing from one of the expedition's planes to build the roof of the hut but weren't certain the hut's walls could support its weight. The tent shown was eventually used to cover the roof of the shelter, offering the men marginal protection from the elements. The crew also tried to construct a rudimentary stove from the engine cowling of one of the planes to heat the inside of the hut but eventually traded the Inuit family who lived next to them a pair of binoculars for a tin stove, which was more suited to the task.

charge, and I will act as an arbiter in the event of any disagree-
ment between him and any of you."

He stopped and looked carefully at the men and tried to
smile.

"We must plan for the worst and hope for the best. If we can
maintain our discipline, we can easily survive this."

Knowing that idleness and boredom could test the sanity of
even the hardiest men, Baker immediately began giving orders,
putting Pearce in charge of the rations while the rest of the men
scoured the surrounding terrain for twigs and sticks for a fire
and rocks and moss for a shelter. Over the next six days, the
party worked hard to stay busy and to finish their makeshift
cabin. In Canada's North, winter came early, and already the
temperatures were tickling the freezing mark. Ice floes began to
form on the surface of the lake, and snow began to fall in the
late afternoons and evenings. At night, the crews huddled in
their sleeping bags, teeth chattering against the northern cold,
sleeping little, alone with the fear that they could die in this
barren wasteland.

Six days later, on September 18, the shelter was finished.
Long and wide enough to accommodate all eight men, the ceiling was a mere five feet high, so no one could stand upright
inside. Goodwin and Milne thought about using one of SK's
wings as a roof, but the weight of the wing threatened to col-
lapse the teetering walls of the flimsy shelter. They elected,
instead, to stretch a canvas tarp over the top.

They also removed the engine cowling of SK and fashioned
a makeshift stove from it, but it proved inefficient for cooking.
MacAlpine traded a set of field glasses to Joe for a proper tin
stove, which the men fed with moss, twigs and fuel from their
planes. The Inuit also gave them food, mostly dried whitefish
and salmon. But the fish was old and rancid, and most of the
party suffered painful stomach cramps and diarrhea after

consuming it. But they had little choice. Without food, they stood no chance of surviving until help arrived.

The men begged and pleaded with Joe to take them to the nearest outpost in his canoe, but Joe would not hear of it. In the North, winter came much earlier than it did in other parts of the country. Joe managed to explain through wild hand gestures and sand sketches that it was too dangerous to canoe anywhere at that time. Most of the waters were starting to freeze over, he explained by pointing to the thin layer of ice beginning to form around the pontoons of the planes. They could become stuck in the ice if they tried to go by canoe at this time of year.

On September 20, a party of two more Inuit arrived at the camp, one of whom spoke passable English. The expedition members nicknamed him "Charlie." Charlie informed the men they had landed on Queen Maud Gulf, on the south side of the Dease Strait. Across the waters of the strait lay Victoria Island and Cambridge Bay. But Charlie agreed with Joe that a crossing by canoe was too risky.

"Better you wait until ice comes," said Charlie. "Then we take you across ice to Cambridge Bay."

"When will that be?" Pearce asked.

"A while still," Charlie replied, smiling. "Colder is better."

The men retired to their "cabin" that evening and lay in the glow of the tin stove, each man pondering the immediate future—a one-month wait, a 70-mile trek across open ice. With each passing day that they didn't hear the drone of another airplane engine, the men slowly lost hope that they would be rescued anytime soon. They worried for their lives and for their families, who had no idea what had happened to them.

They slept late the next morning, trying to conserve their strength. When Tommy crept out of the shelter to respond to nature's call, something seemed off. He looked in the direction of the Inuit camp and saw no dogs, no sled and no movement. A set of tracks led off to the west.

Further inspection of the camp confirmed it. The Inuit had left without a word. MacAlpine and his men were truly alone.

⋘◆⋙

Search Party
September 23, 1929

With each passing day, the staff at Dominion Explorers in Winnipeg became increasingly nervous.

By September 23, they'd received no word from the Mac-Alpine party in more than two weeks. On September 8, the office had received a message from Tommy Thompson:

"Arrived Baker Lake, machine and engine fine. Leaving in morning for Bathurst."

Since then, nothing. No message had been received from the party or from anyone else along the route.

The Colonel left instructions with his staff that, in the event they did not hear from the party for 10 days, they were to mount a search along the flight path. Giving the party an extra five days just to be certain, the staff at Dominion Explorers organized what was the largest aerial search in the history of Canadian aviation.

The next day, General David Hogarth, a friend of the Colonel's for many years, arrived in Winnipeg and began throwing orders around like spare change to organize the search. He set up a headquarters at the Grain Exchange Annex and sent calls for assistance to all other air freight companies with local offices—Western Canada Airways, Consolidated Smelters and Northern Aerial Mineral Exploration, the pet project of Doc Oaks. Guy Blanchet, a representative of Dominion Explorers who had much experience traveling the Arctic, took over the search once he arrived in Winnipeg. Hogarth helped him as much as he could. Each company volunteered pilots, planes and supplies, intent on finding the men of the MacAlpine party and bringing them safely home.

The first person to volunteer for the search was the last flyer to see the party alive, Roy Brown. The famed WWI flying ace could not stomach the thought of his friends and comrades stranded out in the barrens of the Northwest Territories. He resolved that he would do everything in his power to bring the eight men back home to their families.

On September 25, Brown and Bertie Hollick-Kenyon left Winnipeg for Stony Rapids, the launch point of the aerial search. Working on the assumption that the planes had become frozen on a lake because of the cold weather, Brown and Hollick-Kenyon followed their original flight plan, landing at Beverley Lake on the 26th. They found the fuel cache at Beverley Lake drained, confirming that both expedition planes had landed there. It wasn't much to go on—thousands of miles of wasteland still yawned before them—but it was a start.

Roy and Bertie continued on to Baker Lake, planning to hop from there to Bathurst Inlet. But they had few supplies with them, and none was available at Baker Lake. Forced to wait until a supply ship arrived with more fuel and rations, Brown and Hollick-Kenyon continued to make short flights in and around the Baker Lake area with their remaining fuel, but found nothing. Later, two more Dominion Explorers flyers joined them. Bill Spence and Charles Sutton were supposed to have met the MacAlpine expedition at Stony Rapids on September 20. The party never arrived, and upon hearing of the search, both Spence and Sutton volunteered to help out.

The rescuers also received help from a flying legend. Punch Dickins volunteered to aid in the search. He had flown Pearce and MacAlpine across the Barren Lands not a year earlier and had been stranded there with them as well, so he felt an intense desire to help find them. From the 28th to 30th, Dickins and engineer Lew Parmenter flew from Fort Simpson to

Coronation Gulf, the farthest north a plane had yet flown in Canada. They scoured 1500 miles of open land and picked up two prospectors who had been waiting for the MacAlpine party but found no sign of the lost flight crews.

Fortunately, the weather was on their side. But as October loomed, the rescue party had yet to reach Bathurst Inlet. Continually delayed by snow and wind, the men could feel anxiety growing as the weather worsened and they heard nothing from their friends. They knew if they tried to fly in this weather, they could end up lost as well. They could do nothing but wait until the weather cleared.

EXPEDITION
OCTOBER 1, 1929

The Colonel climbed back into the cabin and slumped down onto his sleeping bag.

"It's not getting any colder," he grumbled quietly to Major Baker so that the other men couldn't hear him. "I just threw a rock out onto the lake; it went right through the bloody ice."

Baker nodded, surveying the men. Most were still in their sleeping bags, snoring softly in the late morning. Pearce was awake, counting out the rations for the day and taking a quick inventory of the remaining food. He dropped his notebook and pencil and exhaled loudly, catching the Colonel's eye. He didn't need to say anything. MacAlpine knew they were running out of food.

Lack of food was beginning to show on the men. They had all lost weight, some more than others. Broadway, the mining engineer, didn't have much meat on him to begin with, and the man looked almost skeletal.

The food from the Inuit helped to supplement their own stores, but the men still had problems stomaching the rancid, dried fish and whale blubber. They had all become violently ill more than once in the last week after consuming something the Natives had given them.

Despite the poor quality of their food, the men could not deny their new friends' compassion. They'd all been scared, even angry when their neighbors had just picked up and left in the middle of the night with no notice. But the Natives had returned the next day after hiking to one of their own food caches several miles away to retrieve fish, meat and new furs for the stranded expedition members to wear. They shared what they could, and the McAlpine's men were truly grateful.

When they felt well enough, some of the crew hunted. In the first few weeks, they had shot several ptarmigan, which made for tasty eating. But as the seasons changed, the birds disappeared, and the men could find only squirrels. They set up a net in the waters of Queen Maud Gulf, but the salmon had run months earlier, so they caught only two fish. Pearce promised his pocket watch to the first Inuit to shoot a caribou, but so far they had no luck.

Baker worked his jaw back and forth as he spoke with the Colonel, testing it with his tongue. He had developed a painful abscessed tooth almost a week earlier. He'd been in such agony that Pearce finally held the man down and lanced the abscess with his pocketknife. Pearce had even been thoughtful enough to sterilize the knife in some of the crew's rum before attempting the surgery.

"Damn waste of rum," Goodwin grumbled.

MacAlpine crawled out of the tent, rifle in hand, and began to scour the surrounding wilderness for signs of animal life. Seeing nothing, he made his way over to the Inuit camp to talk to Charlie about what they could expect from the weather. He stuck his head inside the cabin and knocked, then swore so loudly his own men scrambled from their sleeping bags to see what was going on.

Members of the MacAlpine party (from left): Colonel C.D.H.
MacAlpine, Captain Stan McMillan, E.A. Broadway, Alex J.
Milne, Major G.A. (Tommy) Thompson, A.D. Goodwin,
Richard Pearce, Major Robert. F. Baker

~✕~

"Goddammit!" the Colonel shouted, resisting the urge to
hurl the rifle into the lake. "They're gone again!"

A quick search confirmed it—no dogs, no people and lots of
tracks leading west. The men all stared at one another silently,
unsure what to make of it. The last time they'd left, the Natives
returned the next day with supplies. Maybe they were doing
that again.

But the next day came, and the Natives did not return, nor
did they come for the next several days. The condition of the
men worsened considerably; their skin became sallow and
pale; all were tired, lightheaded and queasy. No game could
be found, not a squirrel, let alone a caribou, and their rations
were dwindling quickly. The men spent most of their days and
nights in their sleeping bags or curled around the tin stove,

trying to suck up as much heat as possible. They seldom spoke, too tired and too despondent to bother. They no longer hoped for rescue from the skies but concerned themselves only with getting through the day.

On the morning of October 12, one month after being stranded on the shores of Queen Maud Gulf, Major Baker awoke to a rustling outside the cabin. He held a finger to his lips as the rest of the men stirred, not wanting to scare away whatever animal might be outside. They needed food desperately, and at this point, would have to live off whatever they could find.

Baker grabbed the rifle and slowly crept out of his sleeping bag, making for the door of the cabin. Moving slowly, softly, he stuck his head out the entrance and came face to foot with a pair of moccasins.

Baker looked up at Charlie, who was smiling.

"Hungry?" Charlie asked, and he dropped a large fur sack in front of Baker's face. Inside the bag was more food. Besides fish, the Inuit had been able to hunt down a caribou and had portioned off a generous chunk for their "guests."

Pearce handed over his pocket watch without a word. That night, the men feasted on caribou. Most fell ill the next morning, but they felt stronger, more energetic than they had in weeks.

Five days later, the temperature dropped dramatically. The men saw the drop as a mixed blessing—they found it more difficult to stay warm, but the colder weather would cause the ice to form sooner so that they could make for Cambridge Bay. The snow fell daily now, and the ice on the gulf grew thicker. Charlie informed MacAlpine that they would be leaving in a few days.

That night, 16 more Inuit arrived at the camp, a motley assortment of men, women and children. They greeted the MacAlpine party excitedly, asking lots of questions and gazing at their planes in wonder. That night, all 28 members of the camp crowded inside the sod and canvas shelter for dinner and fellowship. The heat from the extra bodies was more welcome than anything.

Three days later, Charlie stuck his smiling face inside the cabin.

"Tomorrow we go," he said, then closed the flap and left.

The men sighed in relief and packed their belongings. Pearce loosened up on the rations, allowing the men a little extra food to shore up their strength for their coming march—a 70-mile trek to Cambridge Bay, across open ice. The trip would be rough, but the men took heart in the fact they had survived this long, and marching forward at least had a purpose.

❦

SEARCH PARTY
OCTOBER 20, 1929

With each passing day, the search party grew more and more anxious. Still at Baker Lake because the weather had grounded them earlier, they were now in the middle of freeze-up. The ice forming on the surrounding lakes and rivers meant they could no longer land with pontoons, but the ice was not yet thick enough to handle the weight of their planes with skis. And so they waited, passing the time, working on their planes and making short flights in and around the Baker Lake area.

The weather had been hard on the planes, and one was already out of commission. Jimmy Vance's Fokker was damaged beyond repair thanks to an unseasonably warm, howling gale that had caused the ice on the lake to break up. The cracking ice had tossed Vance's plane about like a toy, snapping the tail of the plane so badly that it was irreparable.

But their search party was larger. Vance and Andy Cruickshank had arrived on October 9, but like the rest, were forced to wait until freeze-up was complete. Each day the pilots rushed out the door of their cabin to check the ice on Baker Lake, and each day they walked away, shaking their heads in frustration. They knew that the longer they waited, the less likely they would find their comrades alive.

On the morning of the October 25, the pilots finally agreed that, although waiting another day or two would be advisable, the ice was thick enough. Leaving Baker Lake in the morning, the planes made it to Burnside River to refuel and set up camp for the night. Spotting an open space on the river, Bill Spence led the search party in for a landing. As the plane's skis touched down on the river, he felt the ice groan under the weight of the plane and immediately pulled back on the stick, increasing power and aborting the landing. Roy Brown also landed and also jammed the throttles to the stops to take off once more. But Cruickshank was not so lucky. Not knowing why Brown and Spence had aborted their landings, Cruickshank alighted on the surface of the river. A mighty crack sounded above the roar of the engine, and the outside world disappeared in a violent spray of ice and water.

Acting quickly, the men scrambled through a hatch above Cruickshank's seat to safety before the plane sank through the ice. Standing on the shore, shivering in the cold, their feet and ankles soaking wet, the crew waited for Brown and Spence to land on the shore and pick them up.

"Isn't this just grand?" Cruickshank asked Bill Nadin, his engineer.

❧❖❧

EXPEDITION
OCTOBER 27, 1929

Tommy watched the two Inuit men fade into the blizzard, heading back the way the party had come. He sighed, feeling a bitter, angry despair in his heart. They were stranded again.

Having come almost two-thirds of the way across the ice in the past week, this was the second time they'd been stopped by thin ice. Their supplies had dwindled so much that all they had left was a few strips of dried fish and food for the dogs. The men were exhausted, frozen and frostbitten, and all were slowly losing hope.

They had covered 25 miles their first day out of Queen Maud Gulf, setting out across the great sheet of ice that lay between them and Cambridge Bay. But the effort had been almost too much that first day. Already malnourished and weakened from over a month of being stranded, the men found the hike an especially difficult one. They fought the wind the whole way; it whipped their faces and stung their eyes and cheeks. The ice of the strait had frozen in great hummocks, enormous hills that the men were forced to climb, pulling sledges of supplies. Even though they'd brought a dog team and sleds, they spent most of their time walking across the Dease Strait.

By the end of the first day, the men looked like the walking dead, frozen and exhausted, too tired to even build proper igloos for the night. As a result, one shelter had collapsed early in the morning, forcing them out of bed to repair it.

For miles around they saw nothing but white. They could no longer see land in any direction around them, and Tommy began to wonder if they were still headed in the right direction. But their guides were confident, so Tommy had little choice but to stumble along behind them, not talking, not even thinking. All he could concentrate on was putting one foot in front of the other, and even that was almost more than his weary mind could handle.

They'd been stopped by thin ice the next day and forced to camp out for two days on the unsheltered expanse of the frozen strait until it was safe to proceed. On October 24, they set out again and covered another 25 miles, only to be stopped by thin ice yet again. With a few days wait ahead, two Natives decided to head back to their original camp for more supplies. All the rest could do was wait.

No one cared about the wind and snow anymore. Everything was cold—toes, fingers and noses. They spent the nights and days huddled in their sleeping bags, staring blankly at the walls of the igloo. They were so close to salvation, but they felt as if they would never get there.

❧❖❧

Search Party
October 27, 1929

The landscape seemed like one unending canvas of white to Roy Brown as he looped and circled his plane in and around the northern shores of the Northwest Territories. Staring out his window, he could see nothing but white.

Shaking his head, he banked left and retraced his flight path, scouring the ground below. Paul Davis, his engineer, stared out the passenger window, but found no sign of the MacAlpine party.

"Where are we?" Brown asked, frustrated.

"Let me check." Davis consulted his map. "We're just coming up on Queen Maud Gulf, south side of the Dease Strait. Other side of the strait is Cambridge Bay."

Brown shook his head again.

"I think we're heading the wrong direction. They would have had to be really lost to make it this far west without landing at Bathurst first."

Davis shrugged, "Anything can happen when you're up in the air, Roy. You know that."

Brown nodded and stared out the window again as he roared over the shoreline of the Queen Maud Gulf. Still nothing.

"Want to turn north, head towards Cambridge?" Davis asked him.

Brown considered that option, looking at his fuel gauge.

"I think we'd better head back," said Brown. "I really don't think we'll find them out here."

Davis nodded his agreement. Brown banked right and headed back to the base at Burnside Lake.

⚬⊱◆⊰⚬

EXPEDITION
NOVEMBER 3, 1929

The men awoke early, just before 5:00 AM. They were cold, sore and tired, but determined.

The two Natives who had gone back for food had returned two days earlier with not only a great bag of rations, but encouraging news. While searching for their supplies at Queen Maud Gulf, they had heard an airplane fly overhead. They had not seen it, but they couldn't mistake the sound.

Buoyed by the news, the men spent the rest of November 1 eating and resting, conserving their strength for the final leg of their trek to Cambridge Bay. They covered another 15 miles on November 2 and set up camp, hopeful that they were still on the right course.

Their guides, as usual, amazed them. Aside from hiking almost 100 miles for supplies to sustain their trip, just that day one of the women, nicknamed "Alice," fell through the ice. It took everyone by surprise, but what was even more surprising was Alice's reaction. She did not panic, did not flail or scream. Instead she lay flat until the men were able to lift her clear of the water. Then, in the middle of a crackling wind that froze the beards of every man of the party, she changed her clothes and continued on as if nothing had happened.

That night, before retiring for the evening, Charlie was clear about what needed to happen the next day. The ice was very thin, Charlie had said. They would have to run the rest of the way to Cambridge Bay.

"No stop," Charlie warned them, waggling a stern finger. "If someone fall in, no stop."

After a short breakfast that morning, with Charlie's warning still fresh in their minds, the party began their final dash across the ice. Although they were running, Tommy swore a child could walk faster. It was more of a stumble, an exhausted canter that covered little ground. The ice turned ominously dark beneath their feet, and each man reached deep inside himself and kept running. The party became separated as the stronger ones quickly outpaced the weaker. Unable to stop and wait, the men continued to run, churning and kicking their way through snowdrifts. Their legs burned and cramped, their sides blazed in pain and their lungs ached with every icy blast of wind, but they didn't stop.

Just after noon, the ice began to thicken noticeably, and the first party collapsed beside the exhausted dog team. In the distance, they saw a ship, flag fluttering in the breeze, moored alongside a cluster of wooden buildings.

Tommy licked the ice in his beard and pulled his aching body off the ice. He was so tired that he stumbled along like a drunk. He fell, got up and fell again. Other unsteady hands hauled him up and propelled him forward.

In the waning daylight, the first party arrived at the gates of Cambridge Bay just after 4:30 PM, much to the surprise and delight of the settlement's population. The last group arrived at 7:30, and all were accounted for. The men were hustled inside for medical attention and a warm fire, but MacAlpine walked up the gangway of the *Bay Maud*, the supply ship docked in the bay, and sat down at the wireless radio set.

With fingers frostbitten and beard dripping, MacAlpine spelled out a message for the home base in Winnipeg: "MacAlpine and party found. All well. Located Cambridge Bay."

That night, the men of the MacAlpine party literally ate themselves sick. Feasting on potatoes, jam, marmalade, breads, cakes and cheeses and washing it down with whiskey, the men ate until they were falling asleep in their seats. They were then divided into billets at the HBC outpost, RCMP station and the *Bay Maud* for a night's rest in real beds.

Just after 2:00 AM, Baker and Pearce awoke hungry. Tiptoeing into the kitchen, they feasted on chocolates and sweets before retiring for the night.

❧◆☙

SEARCH PARTY
NOVEMBER 5, 1929

Everyone was losing heart. The rescue crews had managed only one flight since the end of October because they were grounded by poor weather. They had put their time to good use by devising a way to raise Cruickshank's plane from the waters of the Burnside River. But each day that passed with no news of the MacAlpine party meant they were less likely to find them alive.

On November 5, the weather improved somewhat, and the search party decided to resume its search. Brown walked around his plane, checking it over before he started the day's search. Seeing no mechanical problems, Brown started the plane, while Davis climbed in. He taxied out into the center of the river and was just about to open up the throttles for take-off when Davis touched his arm.

"What the hell is that?" Davis asked.

Brown squinted through the windshield. Through the blowing snow, he made out the frantic gallop of a dog team and an Inuit fellow riding the sled, waving one arm frantically.

Brown cut the engine of the plane and hopped out, wondering what was going on. He could hear the man shouting, but it wasn't until the Inuit pulled his team to a halt not five feet from the plane that they could make out what he was trying to say. It was the greatest news Brown and Davies had ever heard.

"They find 'em!" the Inuit shouted. "They find 'em!"

⊷◆⊶

NOVEMBER 23, 1929

It was all Tommy could do not to scream.

Wrapped in his sleeping bag, Tommy listened to the wind moan outside the tent. Not two weeks earlier, he'd been sleeping in a comfortable bed, gorging himself on food and warming his feet by the fireplace. He'd thought the ordeal was over. And now he was stranded again.

Roy Brown and Bill Spence arrived soon after the MacAlpine party had straggled into Cambridge Bay to pick up the weary, frostbitten group and take them home. The flyers gave the key for SK, which they'd left in the water at Dease Point, to their Native guides and explained that they would be back to retrieve the plane sometime in the next year. They'd left Cambridge on November 7 and made Bathurst that day. Snowed in for another five days, the party left for Fort Reliance on the 12th, eager to get back to their families.

Flying over Musk Ox Lake in Bill Spence's plane, a bad fog had obscured visibility, forcing Spence to land until the haze burned off. When the fog lifted and Spence tried to take off, he forgot to switch to his auxiliary fuel tank. Not five feet in the air, the plane's engine stopped and the aircraft smashed into the ice. The fittings of the plane's skis buckled under the weight of the plane, stranding Tommy yet again.

That had been 11 days ago. They'd set up camp beside the plane, erecting their tents and snaking into their sleeping bags, but Tommy was ready to cry. He just wanted to go home.

They'd shot a fox for food a week earlier, a curious white beast that had been foolish enough to stick its nose inside the tent. But in the middle of winter, there was little else to do but lay around and wait for rescue. And they had waited almost two weeks.

Three days later, Tommy awoke to a loud *whumphf* outside the tent, followed by the roar of an engine. Shooting out of the tent in little more than his long underwear, Tommy danced and shouted with glee as Andy Cruickshank's Fokker taxied towards the stranded crew.

Tommy grabbed only what he could carry as he and Bill piled into the Fokker and buckled in.

"I'd love to get you guys home right away, but we have another stop to make," Cruickshank smiled. "Roy's down, too."

"I don't believe it," Tommy laughed, shaking his head.

"That's the nature of the business," Cruickshank shrugged as he turned back towards his controls. "You just never know what's going to happen. We're all just lucky to be alive."

Tommy laughed. Everyone else in the plane joined in as Cruickshank opened up the throttles and the Fokker soared into the air.

Notes on Sources

Canada's Aviation Hall of Fame. Calgary: Oil City Press Ltd., 1974.

Corley-Smith, Peter. *Barnstorming to Bush Flying: 1910–1930.* Vancouver: Sono Nis Press, 1989.

Ellis, Frank H. *Canada's Flying Heritage.* Toronto: University of Toronto Press, 1954.

Ferguson, Paul William. *The Snowbird Decades: Western Canada's Pioneer Aviation Companies.* Vancouver: Butterworth & Co., 1979.

Foster, J.A. *The Bush Pilots: A Pictorial History of a Canadian Phenomenon.* Toronto: McClelland & Stewart Inc., 1990.

Gilbert, Walter E. and Kathleen Shackleton. *Arctic Pilot.* Toronto: Thomas Nelson & Sons Ltd., 1940.

Godsell, Philip H. *Pilots of the Purple Twilight: The Story of Canada's Early Bush Flyers.* Calgary: Fifth House Ltd., 2002.

Grant, Robert S. *Great Northern Bushplanes.* Surrey: Hancock House Publishers Ltd., 1997.

Hartley, Michael. *The Challenge of the Skies.* Edmonton: Puckrin's Production House Ltd., 1981.

Keith, Ronald. *Bush Pilot with a Briefcase: The Incredible Story of Aviation Pioneer Grant McConachie*. Vancouver: Douglas & McIntyre, 1972.

McCaffery, Dan. *Bush Planes and Bush Pilots*. Toronto: James Lorimer & Company Ltd., 2002.

Milberry, Larry. *Aviation in Canada*. Toronto: McGraw-Hill Ryerson Ltd., 1979.

Moar, Jack and Kitty. *A Collection of Bush Flying Stories*. Victoria, 1991.

Myles, Eugenie L. *Airborned from Edmonton*. Toronto: Ryerson Press, 1959.

Pigott, Peter. *Flying Canucks: Famous Canadian Aviators*. Toronto: Hounslow Press, 1994.

Pigott, Peter. *Flying Canucks II: Famous Canadian Aviators*. Toronto: Hounslow Press, 1997.

Pigott, Peter. *Flying Canucks III: Famous Canadian Aviators*. Toronto: Harbour Publishing, 2000.

Reid, Sheila. *Wings of a Hero: Ace Wop May*. St. Catharines: Vanwell Publishing Ltd., 1997.

Spring, Joyce. *Daring Lady Flyers*. Porters Lake: Pottersfield Press, 1994.

Sutherland, Alice G. *Canada's Aviation Pioneers: 50 Years of McKee Trophy Winners*. Toronto: McGraw-Hill Ryerson Ltd., 1978.

Ward, Max. *The Max Ward Story: A Bush Pilot in the Bureaucratic Jungle*. Toronto: McClelland & Stewart Inc., 1991.

Wheeler, William J. *Skippers of the Sky: The Early Years of Bush Flying*. Calgary: Fifth House Ltd., 2000.

Peter Boer

PETER IS A JOURNALIST, author and history buff who has a consuming fascination with military and aviation history. The beginnings of this enduring curiosity can be traced to his evacuation by air from High Level to Edmonton, apparently out of an impatience to be born. His fascination with flight continued to grow as he did. During one memorable moment, young Peter threw up in the back of a Piper Archer II while flying with his father. By high school, he was known to prefer reading military history books to doing his math homework. He went on to university, where he earned a B.A. in psychology with a minor in history. He subsequently studied journalism at Concordia University in Montréal and now writes for the St. Albert Gazette.

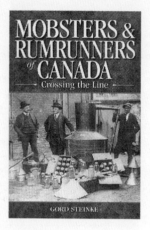
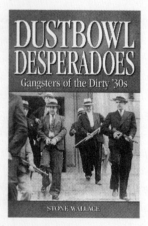

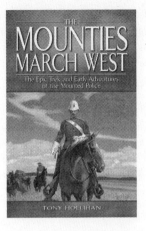

The Mounties March West: The Epic Trek and Early Adventures of the Mounted Police
by Tony Hollihan

The North-West Mounted Police was created in 1873 by Prime Minister John A. Macdonald in order to allow the fledgling nation of Canada to assert its authority over a vast tract of land in the West. They faced a brutal four-month march across a harsh wilderness riding through prairie storms and facing down hostile Natives, starvation, thirst and disease on an epic journey that reduced the proud embodiment of Imperial Britain to a ragtag band of men on the brink of death.

$10.95 US • $14.95 CDN • ISBN 1-894864-04-2 • 5.25"x 8.25" • 240 pages

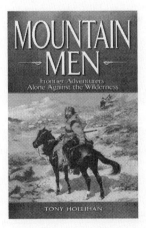

Mountain Men: Frontier Adventurers Alone Against the Wilderness
by Tony Hollihan

An entertaining collection of stories about some of the most colorful of the high-country heroes of North America, those men who explored and trapped on the western frontier. Included are: Kit Carson, Daniel Boone, Davy Crocket, Peter Skene Ogden, Kootenai Brown and more.

$10.95 US • $14.95 CDN • ISBN 1-894864-09-3 • 5.25" x 8.25" • 224 pages

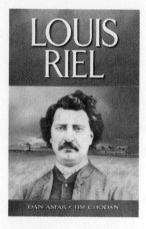

Louis Riel
by Dan Asfar and Tim Chodan
Champion of a people or traitorous revolutionary? Political visionary or religious lunatic? Louis Riel remains one of the most ambiguous figures in Canadian history, a man who stood and fell for the Métis nation. Read about this fascinating western icon in a well-paced biography.

$10.95 US • $14.95 CDN • ISBN 1-894864-05-0 • 5.25" x 8.25" • 232 pages

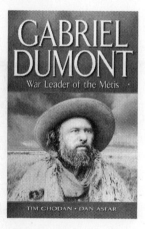

Gabriel Dumont
by Dan Asfar and Tim Chodan
This legendary buffalo hunter and warrior roamed the Canadian plains when buffalo were still plentiful and the Métis ruled the Red River region. The story of Louis Riel's mighty general is recounted here.

$10.95 US • $14.95 CDN • ISBN 1-894864-06-9 • 5.25" x 8.25" • 232 pages

Look for Folklore books at your local bookseller and newsstand or contact the distributor, Lone Pine Publishing, directly. In the U.S. call 1-800-518-3541. In Canada, call 1-800-661-9017.